ISSUES THAT CONCERN YOU

Obesity

Other books in the Issues That Concern You series:

Obesity

Erin Dillon, *Book Editor*

Christine Nasso, *Publisher*
Elizabeth Des Chenes, *Managing Editor*

GREENHAVEN PRESS

An imprint of Thomson Gale, a part of The Thomson Corporation

Detroit • New York • San Francisco • San Diego • New Haven, Conn. • Waterville, Maine • London • Munich

THOMSON
_____✳_____ ™
GALE

© 2007 Thomson Gale, a part of The Thomson Corporation.

Thomson and Star Logo are trademarks and Gale and Greenhaven Press are registered trademarks used herein under license.

For more information, contact
Greenhaven Press
27500 Drake Rd.
Farmington Hills, MI 48331-3535
Or you can visit our Internet site at http://www.gale.com

LIBRARY OF CONGRESS CATALOGING-IN-PUBLICATION DATA
Obesity / Erin Dillon, book editor.
p. cm. — (Issues That Concern You)
Includes bibliographical references and index.
ISBN 0-7377-2194-4 (lib. : alk. paper)
1. Obesity. I. Dillon, Erin. II. Issues That Concern You (San Diego, Calif.)
RC628.O216 2007
616.3'9—dc22
2006041071

Printed in the United States of America

CONTENTS

Jordan Daily has struggled with his weight all of his life. At fifteen he weighed 509 pounds and suffered the cruel teasing of classmates. His weight also prevented him from participating in many activities and sports. "I couldn't fit in the slides on the playground. I couldn't swing 'cause I would break the swings. I couldn't fit in the desks at school. That was really bad 'cause I felt like I was a misfit," he says. Jordan's doctors worried that his obesity was endangering his life. He was prediabetic and suffered from high blood pressure, depression, severe headaches, arthritis, and sleep apnea—a dangerous condition in which patients stop breathing repeatedly in their sleep, sometimes for a minute or longer.

Jordan is one of millions of young Americans struggling with obesity. An estimated 15 percent of children and adolescents from ages six to nineteen are seriously overweight, and many health experts believe that the United States is facing a growing obesity epidemic. The percentage of obese adolescents aged twelve to nineteen has more than doubled since the 1970s, and the prevalence of obesity among children aged six to eleven has nearly tripled. Furthermore, more than 10 percent of preschool children between ages two and five are overweight. This enormous increase in the number of obese young people has become a national concern for many reasons, including the serious health risks of obesity as well as the emotional pain of being extremely heavy in a society that idealizes slimness.

The Health Risks of Obesity

Obese young people face an increased risk for a number of serious diseases, including diabetes, heart disease, stroke, and cancer. As a November 2003 *New York Times* editorial noted, "The issue [of obesity] has long-term implications. For the first time, children are being diagnosed with weight-related chronic ailments that usually strike much later in life, including hypertension and

A group of obese boys enjoy the swimming pool at a camp for overweight youth. Obesity is a growing problem among young Americans.

diabetes." In fact, according to David Ludwig, a doctor at Children's Hospital Boston, the number of young people suffering from Type 2 diabetes has increased tenfold in the past twenty years. These patients are at an increased risk of developing serious and sometimes life-threatening complications of diabetes by the time they are thirty, including kidney failure, heart attack, nerve damage, and blindness. "For a four-year-old or six-year-old who's obese to develop Type 2 diabetes at fourteen or sixteen . . . [is] really a staggering prospect," Ludwig states.

Obese adolescents also face the threat of metabolic syndrome, a group of risk factors that greatly increases a person's chances of developing life threatening chronic diseases. To be diagnosed with metabolic syndrome, a patient must have at least three of the following symptoms:

- A waist size of greater than forty inches for males or thirty-five inches for females
- High blood pressure (greater than 130/85)
- Elevated levels of glucose (blood sugar)
- Low levels of HDL, or "good cholesterol"
- Elevated levels of triglycerides (a type of fat in the bloodstream)

Approximately 1 million young people in the United States already suffer from metabolic syndrome, putting them at great risk for premature heart disease and diabetes. According to the Cleveland Clinic of Health, having the consistently high levels of glucose associated with metabolic syndrome can damage the lining of the arteries, decrease the kidneys' ability to remove salt from the blood (which leads to high blood pressure), increase the risk of blood clot formation, and slow the production of insulin. These dangerous changes to the body all result in an increased risk of developing cardiovascular disease.

The Emotional Toll of Obesity

In addition to the debilitating health consequences of obesity, young people suffering from this condition also face the stigma of being overweight during the often already difficult period of adolescence. This stigma can lead to numerous social and emotional problems. One woman describes the pain she experienced as an obese teenager:

> The first time I ever undressed in the locker room, the other girls laughed and joked and pointed to the rolls and layers of blubber. . . . I never gave them another chance to hurt me like that. From that day on, I always wore my gym shorts and t-shirt under my clothes. My school clothes were a uniform, anyway: stretch pants and a knit top. What did it matter if I added another layer? Not many stylish clothes for teenagers come in size 46 and 48. There were no gym suits large enough to fit me, of course. . . .

Researchers have found that many youngsters are mercilessly teased and bullied because of their obesity.

The isolation and social ostracism many obese teenagers experience can lead to the development of depression or other serious psychological disorders. Researchers at the Centers for Disease Control and Prevention have found that young people who con-

The emotional toll of being overweight shows in the faces of these girls.

Exercising together helps these girls keep a positive attitude while they struggle with their weight issues.

sider themselves extremely overweight are more than twice as likely as their normal-weight classmates to consider or attempt suicide.

Fortunately, some young people struggling with obesity do maintain a positive attitude and offer advice to others who are combating weight problems. Rocky, a fifteen-year-old from Brooklyn who is 6 foot 1 and weighs 393 pounds, states, "Always strive for the best, and basically, you are what you are. Yeah, you have to lose weight. I'm not going to lie and say, 'Oh, weight is good. Keep it on and be happy with it.' You have to come to terms. You have to accept it. You have to start losing weight for you, not for anybody else, but for your health." The physical and emotional cost of obesity is just one of the topics explored in *Issues That Concern You: Obesity*. The authors also investigate the debate over the extent of the obesity epidemic, the role of the fast-food industry in rising obesity rates, and other subjects. In addition, the volume includes a bibliography, a list of organizations to contact for further information, and other useful appendixes. The appendix titled "What You Should Know About Obesity" offers vital facts about obesity and how it affects young people. The appendix "What You Should Do About Obesity" discusses various solutions to the problem of obesity. These many useful features make *Issues That Concern You: Obesity* a valuable resource. Given the growing costs of obesity to society, having a greater understanding of this issue is crucial.

ONE

Obesity Endangers Health

Bonnie Liebman

> In the following viewpoint Bonnie Liebman describes the illnesses associated with obesity, including sleep apnea, diabetes, high blood pressure, and arthritis. She also notes that obesity increases the risk of a variety of cancers. Researchers theorize that obesity raises certain hormone levels, which in turn increases the rate at which cancer cells grow. Although smoking is still the leading cause of cancer in the United States, doctors say that obesity comes in as a close second. Liebman concludes that by losing excess pounds and maintaining a stable weight, people can decrease their risk of developing breast, colon, kidney, and esophagus cancers, as well as protect themselves from a range of other diseases. Liebman is the director of nutrition at the Center for Science in the Public Interest.

If you're like most people, you're at least a few pounds overweight. So what?

Losing weight would lower your risk of diabetes, heart disease, high blood pressure, and arthritis. No surprise there. And it wouldn't hurt the next time you try to squeeze into last year's bathing suit.

Bonnie Liebman, "Fat Chance," *Nutrition Action Health Letter*, vol. 30, October 2003, pp. 1–6. Republished with permission of the *Nutrition Action Health Letter*, conveyed through Copyright Clearance Center, Inc.

What many people don't know is that extra pounds mean an extra risk of cancer—of the breast, colon, esophagus, kidney, uterus, and possibly more.

"We estimate that 90,000 deaths due to cancer could be prevented each year in the U.S. if men and women could maintain normal weight," says Eugenia Calle, director of analytical epidemiology at the American Cancer Society in Atlanta. "After tobacco smoking, obesity is the principal cause of cancer in the U.S.," says Dimitri Trichopoulos of the Harvard School of Public Health.

Suddenly, that spare tire looks more ominous than it did before. Last April [2003], the American Cancer Society (ACS) added more potential cancers when it released the biggest study ever done on excess weight and cancer deaths. (It tracked more than 900,000 people for 16 years.)

"Because it was a very large study, we could look at a wide range of cancers," says lead author Eugenia Calle. The risk of dying of cancers like liver, pancreas, cervix, gallbladder, non-Hodgkin's lymphoma, and multiple myeloma was higher in heavier people. "But we don't have enough data from other studies to know if those links are real," she adds.

The rapidly expanding American waistline contributes to 14 percent of cancer deaths in men and 20 percent in women, says the ACS. That's partly because so many of us are fat. "With something as prevalent as obesity, even a small increase in risk can account for a large number of cancers," says Calle. For most cancers, the fattest people have twice the risk of those who aren't overweight, and the overweight-but-not-obese have only a 20 to 60 percent increased risk. . . .

How do bigger bellies, hips, and thighs lead to tumors? It depends on the cancer, but researchers have a theory that ties at least some of them together.

Mutations or damage to DNA can "initiate" a cancer by turning off normal cell regulation. "But a cancer has to be stimulated to grow," says Calle. That's where obesity comes in. "Obesity raises levels of peptide hormones like insulin and steroid hormones like estrogen," she explains. "Both hormones stimulate cell growth."

Of all the cancers linked to weight, researchers are most interested in the cancer that's most likely to strike women.

Breast Cancer

For years, it looked as though weight had no impact on breast cancer. "We didn't see the effect until we looked only at post-menopausal women who had never been exposed to hormone replacement therapy," explains [Rachel Ballard-Barbash of the National Cancer Institute (NCI)].

In premenopausal women, obesity actually lowers the risk of breast cancer, so that muddied the waters. "It's unclear why weight protects against breast cancer in younger women, at least in affluent countries like the U.S.," says Regina Ziegler, a nutritional epidemiologist at the NCI. One possibility: Obesity interferes with ovulation, and that reduces exposure to estrogen.

But excess weight protects only the heaviest premenopausal women. And those women have a higher risk of diabetes and other illnesses, so "it shouldn't be an excuse to avoid losing weight," Ziegler adds.

Even when researchers looked only at postmenopausal women, weight had little impact on cancer risk . . . until [Harvard researcher Walter] Willett's team excluded women who take hormone replacement therapy. "Women who were taking hormones were at higher risk of breast cancer no matter what their weight, because they were taking pharmacological levels of estrogen," he says.

When he looked at women who were not taking estrogen, the impact of weight was clear. "Obese women had circulating estrogen levels that were three times higher than lean women," says Willett. "That's a huge difference."

For years, researchers have been stumped by the lower rates of breast cancer in Japanese women. "Obesity explains a big piece of the difference between Japan and the U.S.," says Willett. "Almost all Japanese women are in the normal weight range and they don't take hormones."

And it's not just obese women who need to worry. In the American Cancer Society study, the risk of most cancers started to climb at a Body Mass Index (BMI)[1] of 25, which is the dividing line between "normal" and "overweight." But for breast cancer, the risk was higher at the heavier end of the normal range (23.0 to 24.9) than at the leaner end (18.5 to 22.9).

"Many people start out at age 18 with a BMI of 18 or 19," explains Willett. Women who don't gain more weight have the lowest risk of breast cancer. "Women who gain even six to eight pounds have a small increase in risk, and it goes up stepwise from there." . . .

How Could Gaining Weight Affect the Breast?

Overweight postmenopausal women have more estrogen because fat cells convert androgens to estrogen. "In premenopausal women,

---

1. a ratio of a person's height to weight

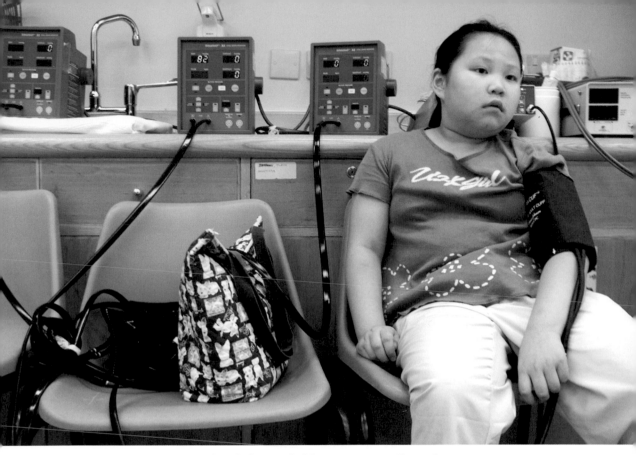

A participant in a study of obese children waits to have her blood pressure taken.

ovaries are the major source of estrogen," explains Ziegler. "But when ovaries stop producing estrogen, the effect of fat cells is more apparent."

Researchers haven't nailed down estrogen as the link between weight and breast cancer, she cautions. "But weight fits right in with the constellation of risk factors for breast cancer," like how many years a woman menstruates, whether she takes replacement estrogen, and how much alcohol she drinks. "They all work by raising circulating hormone levels," says Ziegler. . . .

Scientists don't have proof that women can cut their risk of breast cancer by losing weight, but they're optimistic. "We have every reason to believe that losing weight would reduce risk because we know that risk goes back down when women stop taking estrogen," notes Willett.

What's more, weight loss might lower risk fairly quickly. "In one of our studies, recent weight gain and current weight were the most critical risk factors for breast cancer," says Ziegler. "If women were to adopt lifestyles that lower circulating hormone levels, we might see an impact on breast cancer in five or ten years."

That's not trivial when it comes to a cancer that has few easy-to-change risk factors. "Avoiding weight gain is one of the few things women can do to lower their risk of breast cancer," says Willett. And the impact could be substantial. "If women didn't take estrogen and maintained a healthy weight, it would reduce the incidence of breast cancer by a third and mortality rates by half," he predicts.

It's not just breast cancer. Excess weight also raises the risk of colorectal, esophageal, kidney, and uterine cancer, says the International Agency for Research on Cancer. For other cancers—gallbladder, pancreas, and prostate—the research is less clear.

Colorectal Cancer

Colorectal cancer kills more Americans than any cancer other than lung. High blood insulin levels may be a culprit. "If you're obese, and especially if you carry extra weight around your abdomen, you run the risk of living in a state of high circulating insulin levels," explains the American Cancer Society's Eugenia Calle.

That sets off a chain of events that leads to higher levels of insulin-like growth factors, or IGFs, which promote cell growth. Insulin might also explain why active people have a lower risk. Exercise helps put a lid on insulin levels, even if you're overweight.

Esophageal Cancer

Only 13 out of 100 people survive five years after a diagnosis of esophageal cancer. And the obesity epidemic might explain why one of the two major kinds of esophageal cancer (adenocarcinoma) is on the rise. "Being overweight increases the risk of acid reflux," says Calle.

If acid from the stomach regularly backs up into the lower esophagus, it can eventually cause squamous cells (which usually line the esophagus) to become glandular cells (which usually line the stomach). And that can lead to cancer. "Adenocarcinoma of the esophagus is caused by local acid irritation due to a mass of fat in the abdomen," says Willett.

Gallbladder Cancer

The gallbladder is a small, pear-shaped organ located underneath the liver, just below the right side of your rib cage. The liver makes

A nutrition researcher displays tubes of cancerous tissues used in studies probing possible links between obesity and cancer.

the bile that helps digest fats in the small intestine. The gallbladder concentrates and stores bile.

"Obesity increases the risk of gallstones," explains Calle, "and people who get more gallstones have a higher risk of gallbladder cancer."

Every year, between 6,000 and 7,000 people are diagnosed with gallbladder cancer, and about 3,600 people die of the disease. Most patients are women who are 70 or older.

Kidney Cancer

Kidney cancer is the seventh most common cancer among men and the eleventh most common among women. The odds of surviving five years are 62 percent.

"The cancer is still common and the relationship with obesity is strong," says Willett.

Blood in the urine or a lump near the kidney is the most common symptom, but in its early stages, there may be no symptoms at all.

"Kidney cancer is especially related to abdominal obesity, so insulin may be involved, but we don't really have an explanation," says Harvard's Dimitri Trichopoulos.

Pancreatic Cancer

The pancreas secretes insulin, and the hormone may explain why overweight people seem to have a higher risk. Increased levels of insulin lead to higher levels of insulin-like growth factors (IGF).

"A constellation of factors suggests that IGF may be a factor in pancreatic cancer," says Willett. "But it's difficult to prove one way or the other."

One reason is that pancreatic cancer is such a swift killer. "It's hard to study because people die so soon after they are diagnosed," says the National Cancer Institute's Rachel Ballard-Barbash.

Cancer of the pancreas will strike an estimated 30,700 Americans—and kill 30,000—this year. Only four out of every 100 victims survive for five years.

Prostate Cancer

Overweight men were more likely than normal-weight men to die of prostate cancer in the recent American Cancer Society study. But researchers think that's because excess weight lowers a man's odds of surviving—not getting—the illness.

"When you look at the literature, there's not much evidence that obesity increases the risk of prostate cancer," says Calle. But once a man is diagnosed with the disease, "some studies show a higher risk of either death or advanced disease for overweight men," she adds.

Uterine Cancer

The heaviest women are six times more likely to get cancer of the endometrium (the lining of the uterus) than women who aren't overweight. As with breast cancer, the risk starts to climb even for women who are not yet overweight.

"We saw a higher risk for heavy-normal women than for lean-normal women," says the American Cancer Society's Eugenia Calle.

Estrogen is clearly a culprit, say researchers. "We've known for some time that unopposed estrogen therapy increases the risk of endometrial cancer," says Ballard-Barbash. "Unopposed" means estrogen without progestin.

That's why most women on hormone replacement therapy take both hormones. (Women who've had a hysterectomy take estrogen only.) "Combined estrogen-progestin also increases the risk of endometrial cancer," adds Ballard-Barbash, "but not as much."

The Bottom Line

"Avoiding weight gain, along with not smoking, is one of the most important things people can do to protect their long term health," says Harvard's Walter Willett.

The goal isn't just to keep your BMI in the "normal" range, but to keep your weight stable from your 20s on.

A heavy-normal weight is often not ideal, says Willett. "If you start out with a BMI of 18, you can put on 30 or 40 pounds and still have a BMI under 25." (Roughly every seven pounds moves your BMI up or down one point.) "You're technically in the healthy range, but your weight will increase your risk of breast cancer, as well as diabetes, heart disease, and stroke."

Of course, the "stay lean" message is a little late for many people. But the "lose weight" message isn't, especially when shedding excess pounds has so many benefits beyond cancer.

"You're buying a decreased risk for diabetes, heart disease, hypertension—almost every disease in the book," says the National Cancer Institute's Regina Ziegler.

And for some health problems, the weight loss needn't be large. "The impact on diabetes is huge," says Willett. "In our study, women who reported losing only about ten pounds lowered their risk of diabetes by 80 percent."

With regular exercise, an overweight teen reduces his chances of developing diabetes, heart disease, and cancer.

Could fear of cancer motivate people to lose weight where other diseases have failed?

"Cancer scares people more than heart disease so it may make a difference," says Trichopoulos. But it's not going to be easy.

"Eating is a response to stress and it's one of the few predictable pleasures in life," he adds. "Love and children are pleasures, but they're not predictable. Food is right there." His advice for the overweight: "Cut whatever you're eating by 30 percent."

People also need to see through the food industry's attempts to fatten us up. "We have to break free from 'all-you-can-eat-for-$2.99,'" says Calle. "We need to grab the bull by the horns if we want to turn this problem around."

Do chubby people have a higher risk of cancer?

"The evidence is very strong for a number of cancer sites," says Walter Willett, who chairs the nutrition department at the Harvard School of Public Health.

The plumpest people have a higher risk of cancers of the breast, colon, esophagus, kidney, and uterus, according to the World Health Organization's International Agency for Research on Cancer.

"We've been trying to get that information out to the public," says Willett.

TWO

The Dangers of Obesity Have Been Exaggerated

Paul Campos

In the following viewpoint Paul Campos argues that the dangers associated with obesity may be exaggerated. Overeating and inactivity can contribute to obesity and are health risks, but there is little evidence that obesity alone is unhealthy, Campos writes. A person who is overweight, eats a balanced diet, and exercises may be healthier than a thin person who eats junk food and is inactive. Studies show that people who are at a "normal" weight are no healthier than those who are somewhat obese. In fact, people who are sedentary, whose weight fluctuates from dieting, or who take diet pills have a higher mortality rate than those who are overweight and involved in light physical activity. Rather than succumb to fad diets in order to achieve a supposedly ideal weight, Campos maintains, people should instead eat better, exercise more, and stop obsessing about being thin. Campos is a professor at the University of Colorado School of Law and is the author of *The Obesity Myth: Why America's Obsession with Weight Is Hazardous to Your Health.*

The latest figures indicate that 65 percent of the adult population—more than 135 million Americans—is either "overweight" or "obese." And government officials are increasingly eager to declare America's burgeoning waistline the nation's number-one public health problem. The Surgeon General's recent *Call to Action to Prevent and Decrease Overweight and Obesity* labels being fat an "epidemic" that kills upward of 300,000 Americans per year.

Such declarations lend our obsession with being thin a respectable medical justification. But are they accurate? A careful survey of medical literature reveals that the conventional wisdom about the health risks of fat is a grotesque distortion of a far more complicated story. Indeed, subject to exceptions for the most extreme cases, it's not at all clear that being overweight is an independent health risk of any kind, let alone something that kills hundreds of thousands of Americans every year. While having a sedentary lifestyle or a lousy diet—both factors, of course, that can contribute to being overweight—do pose health risks, there's virtually no evidence that being fat, in and of itself, is at all bad for you. In other words, while lifestyle is a good predictor of health, weight isn't: A moderately active fat person is likely to be far healthier than someone who is svelte but sedentary. What's worse, Americans' (largely unsuccessful) efforts to make themselves thin through dieting and supplements are themselves a major cause of the ill health associated with being overweight—meaning that America's war on fat is actually helping cause the very disease it is supposed to cure.

| BMI Guidelines ||
Classification	Body Mass Index
Underweight	less than 18.5
Normal	18.5 – 24.9
Overweight	25.0 – 29.9
Obese	30.0 – 39.9
Extremely Obese	40.0 or higher

Source: National Institutes of Health, www.nih.gov.

A Flawed Formula for Determining Obesity

The most common way researchers determine whether someone is overweight is by using the "body mass index" (BMI), a simple and rather arbitrary mathematical formula that puts people of varying heights and weights on a single integrated scale. According to the government, you're "overweight" (that is, your weight becomes a significant health risk) if you have a BMI figure of 25 and "obese" (your weight becomes a major health risk) if your BMI is 30 or higher. A five-foot-four-inch woman is thus labeled "overweight" and "obese" at weights of 146 pounds and 175 pounds, respectively; a five-foot-ten-inch man crosses those thresholds at weights of 174 pounds and 210 pounds. Such claims have been given enormous publicity by, among other government officials, former Surgeons General C. Everett Koop—whose Shape Up America foundation has been a leading source for the claim that fat kills 300,000 Americans per year—and David Satcher, who in 1998 declared that America's young people are "seriously at risk of starting out obese and dooming themselves to the difficult task of overcoming a tough illness." . . .

Yet, despite the intense campaign to place fat in the same category of public health hazards as smoking and drug abuse, there is in fact no medical basis for the government's BMI recommendations or the public health policies based on them. The most obvious flaw lies with the BMI itself, which is simply based on height and weight. The arbitrariness of these charts becomes clear as soon as one starts applying them to actual human beings. As *The Wall Street Journal* pointed out last July [2002], taking the BMI charts seriously requires concluding that Brad Pitt, George Clooney, and Michael Jordan are all "overweight," and that Sylvester Stallone and baseball star Sammy Sosa are "obese." . . .

To be sure, even if the BMI categories can be spectacularly wrong in cases such as those involving professional athletes, they're often a pretty good indicator of how "fat" most people are in everyday life. The real question is whether being fat—as determined by the BMI or by any other measure—is actually a health risk. To answer this question, it's necessary to examine the epidemiological evidence. Since the measurable factors that affect whether someone contracts any particular disease or condition can easily number in the hundreds or thousands, it's often difficult to distinguish meaningful data from random statistical noise. And, even where there are clear correlations, establishing cause and effect can be a complicated matter. If researchers observe that fat people are more prone to contract, say, heart disease than thin people, this fact by itself doesn't tell them whether being fat contributes to acquiring

Baseball player Sammy Sosa would be deemed obese by the body mass index, proving that it is not an absolute indicator of obesity.

heart disease. It could easily be the case that some other factor or set of factors—i.e., being sedentary or eating junk food or dieting aggressively—contributes both to being fat and to contracting heart disease.

Unfortunately, in the world of obesity research these sorts of theoretical and practical complications are often dealt with by simply ignoring them. The most cited studies purporting to demonstrate that fat is a major health risk almost invariably make little or no attempt to control for what medical researchers refer to as "confounding variables." For example, the research providing the basis for the claim that fat contributes to the deaths of 300,000 Americans per year—a 1999 study published in the *Journal of the American Medical Association* (JAMA)—did not attempt to control for any confounding variables other than age, gender, and smoking.

Physical activity is a big part of good health, as these girls are learning in a yoga class at a camp for overweight youth.

And, even among studies—such as the *JAMA* one—that ignore variables such as diet or activity levels, there is tremendous disagreement: For every study that indicates some sort of increased health risk for people with BMI figures between 25 and 30 (a category that currently includes more than one out of every three adult Americans), another study indicates such people enjoy lower overall health risks than those whom the government and the medical establishment have labeled "ideal-weight" individuals (i.e., people with BMI figures between 18.5 and 24.9). . . .

Conflicting Studies

What accounts for the conflict between studies that claim being "overweight" is a significant health risk and those that suggest such weight levels might actually be optimal? The biggest factor is that researchers fail to point out that, in practical terms, the differences in risk they are measuring are usually so small as to be trivial. For example, suppose that Group A consists of 2,500 subjects and that over the course of a decade five of these people die from heart attacks. Now suppose that Group B consists of 4,000 subjects and that five members of this group also die from heart attacks over the same ten-year span. One way of characterizing these figures is to say that people in Group A are subject to a (implicitly terrifying) 60 percent greater risk of a fatal heart attack than those in Group B. But the practical reality is that the relevant risk for members of both groups is miniscule. Indeed, upon closer examination, almost all studies that claim "overweight" people run significantly increased health risks involve this sort of interpretation (or, less generously, distortion) of their data.

This phenomenon is in part a product of the fact that studies that purport to find significant elevations of mortality risk associated with different weight levels usually focus on mortality rates among relatively young adults. Since these studies typically involve very small numbers of deaths among very large numbers of subjects, it isn't surprising to see what appear to be large oscillations in relative risk across different studies. Indeed, one often observes large, apparently random oscillations in risk even within studies.

Lost in the uproar over the *JAMA* study's 300,000 deaths figure is the peculiar fact that the report actually found that supposedly "ideal-weight" individuals with a BMI of 20 had essentially the same mortality risk as "obese" persons with BMI figures of 30 and that both groups had a slightly higher mortality risk than "overweight" people with BMI figures of 25.

In short, the Cornell survey of the existing literature merely confirmed what anyone who actually examines the data will discover: In a decided majority of studies, groups of people labeled "overweight" by current standards are found to have equal or lower mortality rates than groups of supposedly "ideal-weight" individuals. . . .

Overweight and Healthy

As we have seen, most of the people the government and the health establishment claim are too fat—those categorized as "overweight" or "mildly obese"—do not in fact suffer from worse health than supposedly "ideal-weight" individuals. It is true that some groups of fat people—generally those with BMI figures well above 30—are less healthy than average, although not nearly to the extent the anti-fat warriors would have you believe. (Large-scale mortality studies indicate that women who are 50 or even 75 pounds "overweight" will on average still have longer life expectancies than those who are 10 to 15 pounds "underweight," a.k.a. fashionably thin.) Yet there is considerable evidence that even substantially "obese" people are not less healthy because they're fat. Rather, other factors are causing them to be both fat and unhealthy. Chief among these factors are sedentary lifestyle and diet-driven weight fluctuation.

The most comprehensive work regarding the dangers of sedentary lifestyle has been done at the Cooper Institute in Dallas. The institute's director of research, Steven Blair, is probably the world's leading expert on the relationship between activity levels and overall health. For the past 20 years, the Cooper Institute has maintained a database that has tracked the health, weight, and basic fitness levels of tens of thousands of individuals. . . . It turns

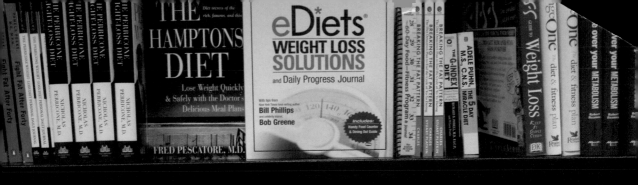

The American obsession with weight loss can be seen in the profusion of weight-loss pills (inset) and diet books crowding store shelves.

out that "obese" people who engage in moderate levels of physical activity have radically lower rates of premature death than sedentary people who maintain supposedly "ideal-weight" levels.

For example, a 1999 Cooper Institute study found the highest death rate to be among sedentary men with waist measurements under 34 inches and the lowest death rate to be among physically fit men with waist measurements of 40 inches or more. And these results do not change when the researchers control for body-fat percentage, thus dispensing with the claim that such percentages, rather than body mass itself, are the crucial variables when measuring the health effects of weight. Fat people might be less healthy if they're fat because of a sedentary lifestyle. But, if they're fat and active, they have nothing to worry about.

Still, even if it's clear that it's better to be fat and active than fat and sedentary—or even thin and sedentary—isn't it the case that being thin and active is the best combination of all? Not according to Blair's research: His numerous studies of the question have found no difference in mortality rates between fit people who are fat and those who are thin. . . .

Other researchers have reached similar conclusions. For instance, the Harvard Alumni Study, which has tracked the health

Like many Americans, this young man adds to his weight problems by eating junk food and watching TV.

of Harvard graduates for many decades, has found the lowest mortality rates among those graduates who have gained the most weight since college while also expending at least 2,000 calories per week in physical activities. Such work suggests strongly that when obesity researchers have described the supposed health risks of fat, what they have actually been doing is using fat as a proxy— and a poor one at that—for a factor that actually does have a significant effect on health and mortality: cardiovascular and metabolic fitness. As Blair himself has put it, Americans have a "misdirected obsession with weight and weight loss. The focus is all wrong. It's fitness that is the key."

The Dangers of Dieting

If fat is ultimately irrelevant to health, our fear of fat, unfortunately, is not. Americans' obsession with thinness feeds an institution that actually is a danger to Americans' health: the diet industry.

Tens of millions of Americans are trying more or less constantly to lose 20 or 30 pounds. (Recent estimates are that, on any particular day, close to half the adult population is on some sort of diet.) Most say they are doing so for their health, often on the advice of their doctors. Yet numerous studies—two dozen in the last 20 years alone—have shown that weight loss of this magnitude (and indeed even of as little as ten pounds) leads to an increased risk of premature death, sometimes by an order of several hundred percent. By contrast, over this same time frame, only a handful of studies have indicated that weight loss leads to lower mortality rates—and one of these found an eleven-hour increase in life expectancy per pound lost (i.e., less than an extra month of life in return for a 50-pound weight loss). This pattern holds true even when studies take into account "occult wasting," the weight loss that sometimes accompanies a serious but unrelated illness. For example, a major American Cancer Society study published in 1995 concluded in no uncertain terms that healthy "overweight" and "obese" women were better off if they didn't lose weight. In this study, healthy women who intentionally lost weight over a period of a year or longer suffered an all-cause increased risk of premature mortality that was up to 70 percent higher than that of healthy women who didn't intentionally lose weight. Meanwhile, unintentional weight gain had no effect on mortality rates. (A 1999 report based on the same data pool found similar results for men.) The only other large study that has examined the health effects of intentional weight loss, the *Iowa Women's Health Study*, also failed to find an association between weight loss and significantly lower mortality rates. In fact, in this 42,000-person study, "overweight" women had an all-cause mortality rate 5 to 10 percent lower than that of "ideal-weight" women. . . .

The grim irony lurking behind these statistics is that, as numerous studies have demonstrated, people who lose weight via dieting and diet drugs often end up weighing a good deal more than people of similar initial weight who never diet. The explanation for this perverse result can be found in the well-documented "set-point" phenomenon—that is, the body's tendency to fight the threat of starvation by slowing its metabolism in response to a caloric reduction. For example, obesity researcher Paul Ernsberger has done several studies in which rats are placed on very low-calorie diets. Invariably, when the rats are returned to their previous level of caloric intake, they get fat by eating exactly the same number of calories that had merely maintained their weight before they were put on diets. The same is true of human beings. "Put people on crash diets, and they'll gain back more weight than they lost," Ernsberger has said. . . .

Americans' Aversion to Obesity

What is it about fat that renders so many otherwise sensible Americans more than a little bit crazy? The war on fat is based on many things: the deeply neurotic relationship so many Americans have developed toward food and their bodies, the identification of thinness with social privilege and of fat with lower-class status, the financial interests of the diet industry, and many other factors as well. Ultimately, the fundamental forces driving our national obsession with fat fall into two broad and interrelated categories: economic interest and psychological motivation.

Obesity research in the United States is almost wholly funded by the weight-loss industry. For all the government's apparent interest in the fat "epidemic," in recent years less than 1 percent of the federal health research budget has gone toward obesity-related research. (For example, in 1995, the National Institutes of Health spent $87 million on obesity research out of a total budget of $11.3 billion.) And, while it's virtually impossible to determine just how much the dieting industry spends on such research, it is safe to say that it is many, many times more. Indeed, many of

A trip to the beach shows that people naturally come in different shapes and sizes, some thinner, some fatter.

the nation's most prominent obesity researchers have direct financial stakes in companies that produce weight-loss products. . . .

So what should we do about fat in the United States? The short answer is: nothing. The longer answer is that we should refocus our attention from people's waistlines to their levels of activity. Americans have become far too sedentary. It sometimes seems that much of American life is organized around the principle that people should be able to go through an average day without ever actually using their legs. We do eat too much junk that isn't good for us because it's quick and cheap and easier than taking the time and money to prepare food that is both nutritious and satisfies our cravings.

A rational public health policy would emphasize that the keys to good health (at least those that anyone can do anything about—genetic factors remain far more important than anything else) are, in roughly descending order of importance: not to smoke, not to be an alcoholic or drug addict, not to be sedentary, and not to eat a diet packed with junk food. It's true that a more active populace that ate a healthier diet would be somewhat thinner, as would a nation that wasn't dieting obsessively. Even so, there is no reason why there shouldn't be millions of healthy, happy fat people in the United States, as there no doubt would be in a culture that maintained a rational attitude toward the fact that people will always come in all shapes and sizes, whether they live healthy lives or not. In the end, nothing could be easier than to win the war on fat: All we need to do is stop fighting it.

THREE

The Acceptance of Obesity Is a Dangerous Trend

Jennifer Grossman

In the following viewpoint Jennifer Grossman contends that organizations such as the National Association to Advance Fat Acceptance (NAAFA), which advocates that overweight people should accept their bodies rather than attempt to lose pounds by dieting or exercising, are in dangerous denial of the health risks of obesity. Grossman writes that NAAFA arbitrarily rejects widely accepted findings linking obesity to health problems such as diabetes, osteoporosis, and heart disease. Members are instead urged to resist dieting and succumbing to American culture's fixation on having a thin body. Activists have valid concerns about the discrimination overweight people face, Grossman argues. However, she contends that their attempts to overturn conventional wisdom concerning nutrition and health make it more difficult for adults to lose weight and, most importantly, make it more likely that children will become obese. By arguing that obesity is completely unrelated to health problems and that overweight people cannot control their size, activists have changed the way that school officials and parents deal with the problem of overweight children. Grossman concludes that many teachers and parents are now afraid to discuss the health risks of obesity, worrying that such discussions could encourage fat phobia. Grossman is the director of the Dole Nutrition Institute.

On my office wall hangs a framed *New Yorker* cartoon of a map of the United States that labels the entire country "Too Fat," save for the dot designating Los Angeles as "Too Skinny." I chose it as a parody both of the field in which I work—health and nutrition—and of the area in which I live: Malibu, California. Camryn Manheim, author of *Wake Up, I'm Fat!*, described Southern California as a place "where people shop for groceries in bikinis." What for fat people are "the two most terrifying things in the world, shopping for food and being practically naked, these sun-soaked creatures do simultaneously."

Which is why I thought this Land of the Lean a curious choice for this year's annual conference of the National Association to Advance Fat Acceptance (NAAFA). I decided to investigate, drawn by both proximity and paradox. A conference premised on persuading people to accept rather than fight their fat seemed not just out of sync with its surroundings, but also out of step with the times.

Not a day goes by without fresh headlines about the prevalence, health risks, and mounting medical costs of obesity. This drumbeat of bad news, however, did nothing to deter those gathered at the LAX Marriott for four days of seminars on such topics as socializing at the pool-side luau and "Ample Hygiene for Ample People." To the extent that these research results were mentioned at all, they were dismissed as further proof of a society conspiring to make fat people feel bad. It put one in mind of what it must have been like to attend a gathering of student Marxists after the fall of the Berlin Wall.

Thus news of the increased risk for cancer, heart disease, birth defects, osteoporosis, and diabetes among the overweight and the obese was greeted with defiance and waved off with denial. Besides, NAAFA members make use of rising weights as an opportunity to redefine normal. As Michael Fumento pointed out in his prophetic book *Fat of the Land* (1997): "The fat activists seem to take great comfort in the growing American waistline, seeing it as both a confirmation and a matter of safety in numbers."

With 2,500 members, NAAFA's numbers—and those of similar groups such as the Body Image Task Force and the Network for Self-Esteem—remain relatively small. The real measure of their success lies in the degree to which society has come around to their point of view. If setting a size-acceptance gathering smack

Loving themselves as fat is the goal of these NAAFA members. However, their slogan (inset) may also deny their potential health risks.

FAT PEOPLE ARE MORE FUN

dab in image-obsessed L.A. seems ironic, it actually represents a dichotomous phenomenon underway across the land. As Americans have grown fatter, two things have occurred: One is the rise of the billion-dollar diet industry, the other is the emergence of a culture of accommodation. The first caters to those who want to lose weight, with advice ranging from the helpful

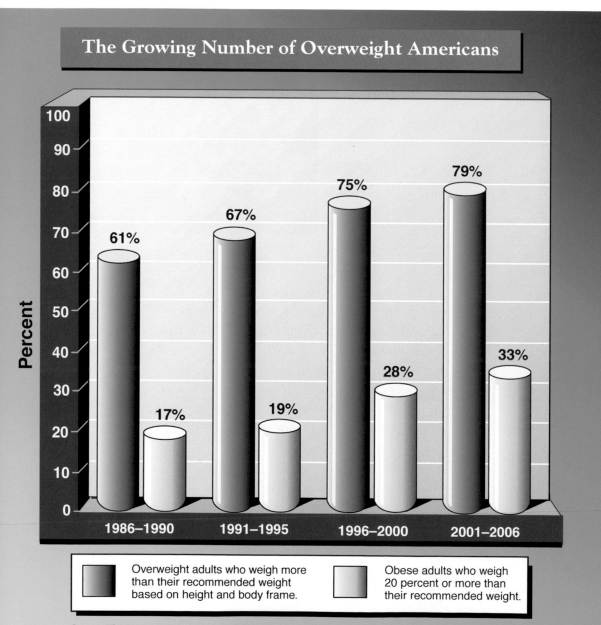

The Growing Number of Overweight Americans

Percent

Year	Overweight	Obese
1986–1990	61%	17%
1991–1995	67%	19%
1996–2000	75%	28%
2001–2006	79%	33%

Overweight adults who weigh more than their recommended weight based on height and body frame.

Obese adults who weigh 20 percent or more than their recommended weight.

Source: The Harris Poll, "Obesity Epidemic Continues to Worsen in the United States," March 9, 2006.

and healthful to the harmful and fraudulent. The second caters to those who despair of losing weight by telling them to drop the guilt, not the pounds. In the lexicon of the latter, restrained eating is invariably described as "starving," gluttony is defended as "enjoying life" (even as it shortens it), and corpulence is euphemized as "curvaceous." Such language may make one feel better about being fat, but only at the cost of perpetuating the choices that helped create the condition.

Being Fat Is Not a Flaw

While fat activists have raised some legitimate concerns—lobbying doctors for wider examination tables, for example, or pressuring car manufacturers to provide seatbelt extensions for the extra-large—their view of fat as fate has undermined both individual efforts to overcome obesity and society's ability to deal with it effectively. The recent spate of fast-food lawsuits took advantage of enduring ambiguity over who bears responsibility for weight gain. At the same time, the equation of weight with other immutable traits, like race, has provided grounds for workplace-discrimination suits. . . .

Though divergent in their aims, both the diet and the anti-diet books employ the same method: mind over matter. The diet books do this by enlisting willpower to lose weight, the anti-diet books by using wishful thinking to dismiss its importance altogether. Similarly, NAAFA endeavors to advance acceptance by retreating from reality. Upon registering for the conference, I entered a world in which "fat people are far less likely to get almost every form of cancer than thin people" and in which dieting—not poor food choices or overeating—is the real cause of weight gain. For those who found their grip on unreality slipping, there was a refresher seminar entitled "Relapse Prevention for Recovered Dieters" to help them guard against those moments of weakness "when weight loss looks seductive." . . .

For my first seminar I was torn between a "Chair Dancing" class and a session entitled "Worth Your Weight." I chose the latter even though, by that calculation, I was obviously the most worthless member of the group. Our facilitator, Barbara Altman Bruno,

Ph.D., author of *Worth Your Weight*, led the lecture/group-therapy session on attitudes toward fat in modern America and different cultures through the ages—recounting how fat women have been prized in Soviet Russia, Third World Africa, and ancient Egypt. Her point, of course, was that perceptions of beauty are relative rather than absolute, so it makes little sense to "weigh our worth" in scales equilibrated by Madison Avenue. . . .

But Dr. Altman Bruno is correct in a deeper sense. While ideals of beauty may not change that dramatically over the course of our lifetime, our own exteriors—whether lithe or large—will. To set one's self-esteem by how well we match up against the ageless, unlined faces and adolescent bodies that adorn fashion covers is masochistic madness. Fitness, sunscreen, plastic surgery, and hormone therapy may temporarily postpone the inevitable, but unless we can finally bring ourselves to accept what we cannot change—in this case, the passage of time—we are destined to despair. It's only when this axiom is applied to the condition of obesity that I get lost. But belief in density as destiny lies at the heart of fat acceptance. So immutable, in this view, is one's weight, that even to try to change it is as futile and, indeed, dangerous as attempting to alter natural law.

Redefining a "Balanced Diet"

Although "Worth Your Weight" was supposed to be about cultural attitudes toward fat, as I discovered it is impossible to sit through more than 15 minutes of one of these seminars without someone circling back to the evils of dieting. Dr. Altman Bruno told our group, "The best way to develop an eating disorder is to go on a diet, because it makes some foods good and some foods bad."

I thought back to when I was 15 and went on my first diet, and realized she was right. Among my favorite foods at the time were pecan-sandy cookies, butterscotch sundaes, Cheetos, and cream soda. As a result of loving these foods a little too much I found my jeans a little too tight and so began what would become a lifelong habit of reading food labels and counting calories. I learned that, measure for measure, fruits and vegetables had relatively fewer calories whereas cookies and junk food had relatively more—so I could eat all I wanted of the former, but very little of the

An overweight fourteen-year-old tries to change her eating habits by shopping for healthy food.

latter if I wanted to lose weight and keep it off. So, yes, dieting can definitely make some foods good and others bad—and all that we've learned in recent years about fiber and phytochemicals, on one hand, and processed carbohydrates and partially hydrogenated oils on the other, serves to reinforce that distinction.

Such sharp-edged distinctions are unwelcome at NAAFA, where roundness reigns and no food need fear discrimination. But while the all-foods-are-good message is cast into plain relief at a conference where the unhealthy results of alimentary inclusiveness are on ample display, the larger and more important truth is how this message, and other fat-acceptance standards, permeate our culture at large. Indeed, other than the context, there's little difference between Dr. Altman Bruno's message and the culture-wide conventional wisdom that "all foods can be part of a balanced diet."

Obviously, there is literal truth to this argument: No single food is responsible for obesity. Just as obviously, and more importantly, some foods—energy-dense, low-nutrient foods—are more responsible than others. By emphasizing the largely irrelevant assurance that eating foods such as ice cream and potato chips once in a while won't kill you, we obscure the far more fundamental fact that their regular overconsumption ultimately may. . . .

Changing Cultural Values

While the main drivers of this change were agricultural, economic, and technological in nature (e.g., cheap sweeteners, shelf-stable fats, labor-saving inventions), less tangible forces were also at work. Most significantly, mores shifted markedly in a more permissive, self-referential direction, influencing both our outlook and our behavior regarding issues ranging from drugs to sex to divorce. Society's approach to food and body size was not exempt from this drift.

Unfortunately, the very values needed to deal with the rising ubiquity of low-cost, high-calorie foods—namely, self-restraint and delayed gratification—were simultaneously going out of style. Similarly, while the number of new candy, gum, and snack products on the market was increasing tenfold in the two decades after 1980, our approach to child feeding changed as well. The tangible factors responsible for childhood weight gain—e.g., school vending machines, more junk food, and less exercise—have been widely recognized, as has their result. Far less remarked upon is how a simultaneous sea change in cultural values may have contributed to the problem: Namely, how a new laissez-faire [let them do as they please] approach to children's discipline encouraged a laissez-manger [let them eat as they please] approach to their diets as well. . . .

The chief reason to question fat acceptance is not that it makes it harder for fat adults to lose weight, but that it makes it easier for children to gain weight. The more we treat fat as something beyond our control, the more we will candy-coat its consequences, the more parents will be disinclined to set limits on food, the more vulnerable we will leave children to sophisticated food marketing, and the more likely they will be to put on pounds that will potentially doom them to an adulthood of obesity, health problems, and early death.

On my second day at the NAAFA conference, I decided to check out the party line on childhood obesity by attending a seminar called "Save the Kids" with Marilyn Wann, publisher of *FAT!SO?* magazine and author of a book by the same name (of which half the proceeds went to NAAFA's Kids Project to combat fat prejudice in schools). The book made her a celebrity among this crowd, and deservedly so: It's a hilarious how-to guide to surviving being fat with your sense of humor and self-esteem intact, complete with a paper doll of the portly Paleolithic fertility icon Venus of Willendorf, outfitted with a wardrobe of lingerie, workout togs, and dashiki ("for the protest rally").

Wann was the only speaker I heard who made a point of emphasizing the importance of exercise and nutrition (her book contains an ode to broccoli, and her favorite ways of preparing it).

Don Wright. Copyright © by Don Wright. Reproduced by permission.

Weighing almost ninety pounds, this four-year-old is extremely overweight for her age.

Indeed, the reason she is so concerned with the recent spate of new childhood-obesity programs—which she calls "abolish the fat children" programs—is that she fears they may do "more harm than good by reinforcing stigma and poisoning kids against nutrition and exercise." Wann is also of the school that believes parents should "let the child decide how much to eat." . . .

Weight Loss and Motivation

Wann and her fellow fat activists lose credibility, however, when they insist that excess weight is harmless to health. The truth is that emotional trauma is just one of the ways in which obesity hurts children. There are orthopedic problems, such as arthritic joints from overburdened limbs, slipped hips, and Blount's disease, in which the legs bow under excess weight, causing knee pain and limiting mobility. There are respiratory diseases like Pickwickian syndrome—in which shallow breath caused by excess abdominal fat leads to oxygen deprivation—sleep apnea, allergic asthma, and weakened lungs. There is hypertension, high blood pressure, and fatty build-up in the arteries of overweight children—all forerunners of coronary heart disease. And, most prevalently, there is the rise in a disease once thought to afflict only adults: Type 2 diabetes.

Unfortunately, many parents and school officials refuse to talk about these dangers for fear of fostering fat-phobia, or encouraging eating disorders like anorexia nervosa. Never mind that bingeing and compulsive eating are disorders, too. Never mind that the tiny number—epidemiologically speaking—of anorexics and bulimics is dwarfed by the legions of overweight and obese children. (In New York City elementary schools, fully half of schoolchildren are overweight or obese.) Never mind that anorexia afflicts mostly white, upper-middle-class girls, while the children at highest risk for obesity are disproportionately low-income minorities. Only the heartless among us could fail to be moved by the plight of obese children, who, according to a recent study published in the *Journal of the American Medical Association*, rate their quality of life as low as that of children undergoing chemotherapy. But to challenge fat acceptance is not to endorse self-loathing or condone body bigotry. We do our children no favors when we downplay the dangers of obesity in the interest of safeguarding self-esteem. . . .

Can feeling bad about being big be better for your health? One wishes it weren't so. One wishes weight loss were motivated by the desire to "be good to ourselves" rather than by shame, vanity, or the desire to appeal to the opposite sex. One wishes we all exercised out of sheer joy of movement rather than the need to burn calories. One wishes, above all, that we were valued for our inner qualities rather than for the way we look. This is why the blandishments of fat acceptance are so powerful, for they promise to grant such wishes and change unpleasant aspects of reality, not by requiring any effort on our part, but by fiat of make-believe. . . .

Losing Weight Requires a Conscious Choice

Beauty may in the end remain in the eye of the beholder, but the practice of science and medicine relies on the premise of an objective reality in which truths—however unflattering, annoying, or inconvenient—are nonetheless true. In denying basic truths about fat, activists have turned the wisdom of the Serenity Prayer on its head. They urge acceptance of something that can be changed—excess weight—while trying to change what they cannot: the reality of its health risks. Even the most shameless among us would not dare pass off the unlovely wages of other risky behavior—smoker's cough, cirrhosis of the liver, hepatitis C, gonorrhea—as a genetic inheritance, much less a badge of pride. But when the substance abused is food, and when the consequence is corpulence, we are too willing to overthrow common sense in favor of politically correct platitudes like "beauty comes in all shapes and sizes."

To be sure, some of us are born with larger bone structures, or lower metabolisms. But very few of us were born to be obese. We can change how much we exercise and what foods we choose. Unlike acceptance, these choices require effort. For that reason, they promise a far more enduring esteem than that which rests on acceptance alone.

FOUR

Low-Income Americans Face a High Risk of Obesity

Amy Winterfeld

For many families at low-income levels, healthy foods such as fresh fruits and vegetables can be too expensive or difficult to find. Fast food, on the other hand, is cheaper and more readily available. In the following viewpoint Amy Winterfeld argues that many Americans are obese because they are unable to afford low-fat, nutritious foods. She cites a 2004 report in the *American Journal of Clinical Nutrition* that found that the highest obesity rates in the United States are in areas with elevated poverty levels and among people with very little education. The report also noted a trend among low-income families to overeat less healthy, cheaper foods to compensate for the lack of high quality foods. Winterfeld also notes that the health problems resulting from obesity heavily strain state budgets and cost taxpayers millions of dollars through programs like Medicare and Medicaid. To combat these costs and help young people fight obesity, legislators and other community leaders are attempting to make healthy foods more readily available. For example, Texas schools have banned unhealthy items from their breakfast and lunch cafeteria menus and instead offer more nutritious and fresh foods. Winterfeld is a senior policy specialist for the National Conference of State Legislatures.

Amy Winterfeld, "Overfed but Undernourished," *State Legislatures*, April 2005, pp. 34–36. Reproduced by permission.

In the land of plenty, Americans in growing numbers are obese. The reasons seem obvious—consuming too many calories, exercising too little to burn them away. Not necessarily so.

In low-income communities all across the country, the story is more complicated. The laws of thermodynamics haven't changed, but they're more difficult to apply when healthy foods are out of economic reach.

In lower socioeconomic areas, says Texas Commissioner of Agriculture Susan Combs, "there's a dearth of fruits and vegetables reasonably priced. Yet there's cheap fast food. It's certainly understandable why people opt for a burger for their 8-year-old kid."

Healthy choices are often unaffordable even when local markets stock fresh fruits, vegetables and other low fat, nutrient-dense foods. And it takes more time to prepare healthy, fresh foods, which may be difficult for many working poor families. These families also may need to learn what's healthy and how to prepare it.

Preparing Meals on a Low Income

Story after story reports the difficulties of locating, affording and preparing nutritious meals for those living at lower income levels.

In Boston, Robin Smith, a hospital worker, has only $30 to $40 a week to spend on groceries for herself and two daughters. That means she can afford the leaner cuts of meat only when they are on sale and fresh vegetables "once in a blue moon."

In Starr County, Texas, where 59 percent of children live below the poverty level, 24 percent of children are overweight or obese by age four, 28 percent by kindergarten, and by elementary school, 50 percent of boys and 35 percent of girls are overweight or obese. Almost half of the adults in Starr County, the poorest in Texas, have type 2 diabetes, and nearly every child is at risk for the disease because a close relative (parent, sibling, aunt or uncle) is already afflicted.

California farm worker Iris Caballero is overweight and diabetic, but cannot always afford the produce in the state's central valley, which also has some of the nation's highest poverty rates. During harvest season, when she works picking grapes and oranges, Caballero can find and purchase fruit in the local mini-market.

Offers of cheap fast food like this McDonald's burger deal keep many people coming back for more.

In the winter, when work and fruits and vegetables are hard to find, Caballero depends on the cheapest food available to feed her family—potatoes, bread and tortillas.

Untreated diabetes caused the blindness of a 15-year-old student in Caballero's community, but served as the impetus for a free nutrition class for farm workers through the public health program. A rarity, the class offers information that takes into account limited budgets and lack of time while respecting culinary traditions. The local elementary school also offered a class for teachers on how to respond to high and low blood sugar emergencies.

Research reported in the January 2004 *American Journal of Clinical Nutrition* confirms that the highest obesity rates occur among people with the highest poverty rates and the least educa-

Deep-fried chicken strips and fries may be tasty but they are definitely not healthy especially when eaten in large quantities.

tion. Moreover, the research confirms what Smith, Caballero and others like them have learned in practice: lower-calorie, high-nutrient foods cost more per calorie. As a result, many poor families are affected by "food insecurity," that is, the limited or uncertain availability of foods that are nutritionally adequate. These families may overeat to maximize caloric intake for their limited dollars when food is available. In the process, they sacrifice food quality for larger quantities, often resulting in obesity.

Bad for State Budgets

If being svelte was solely a cosmetic issue, policy concerns might not matter. Obesity, however, has a host of health and state budget consequences. About 50 percent of obese children become obese adults. In fact, we may be raising the first generation of American children to live sicker and die younger than their parents. People who don't maintain a healthy weight are at risk for a plethora of serious chronic conditions such as type 2 diabetes, heart disease, stroke, high blood pressure, cancer, and even gallbladder disease and arthritis.

The current impact on state budgets is staggering. It is estimated that in 2003, obesity carried a $75 billion price tag with half paid by taxpayers through Medicare (which covers older Americans with chronic conditions that may be related to obesity) and Medicaid (which primarily serves the poor, who are more likely to suffer from obesity). Estimated obesity-related medical expenditures ranged from $87 million in Wyoming, which included $15 million in Medicare expenditures and $23 million in Medicaid, to $7.7 billion in California, including $1.7 billion each in Medicare and Medicaid.

Making Healthy Food More Widely Available

Legislators are beginning to look not only at how to respond to obesity, but also how to prevent the conditions that contribute to it.

In Pennsylvania, two intertwined bipartisan legislative initiatives are aimed at making healthy foods more available in low-income communities. Spearheaded by Representative Dwight Evans, the Commonwealth's First Industries Fund, an economic stimulus program, now makes supermarkets eligible to receive $150 million in planning grants, loans and loan guarantees in order to promote urban and rural supermarket development.

Pennsylvania's Fresh Foods Financing Initiative, the second effort led by Evans, provided $10 million in state seed money that was matched by $30 million raised from other sources to create a public-private partnership. The initiative's goal is to make nutritious foods more available, but benefits have also included the creation of 258 jobs and development of a huge supermarket that opened in Philadelphia last September [2004]. Evans envisions direct health benefits for his constituents.

"As an African-American legislator, I'm very concerned about the issues of diabetes and cancer," he says. "Bringing quality food outlets to inner-city neighborhoods is a way to encourage healthy nutrition choices to fight those diseases. It's also an economic engine driver—it builds businesses, it generates jobs, it transforms communities. All of those things are part of this initiative."

Encouraging Better Nutrition in Schools

Other states are considering policies to encourage better food choices, especially in schools. Texas Commissioner Susan Combs notes there were 7,000 diabetes-related amputations last year [2004] in her state. And children are showing signs of the disease at age 8 or 9; some 15-year-olds already have type-2 diabetes. If these unhealthy trends continue, says Combs, coupled with an aging population and population growth, "from the most cold-blooded economic standpoint, the medical costs will break the state." She has become a strong advocate of making healthy foods available in all schools.

In Combs' view, the state stands in loco parentis [in place of the parent] during the school day and is responsible for setting a good example by offering only healthy food. "Your state makes them go to school. You must do them no harm while they're in your care," says Combs.

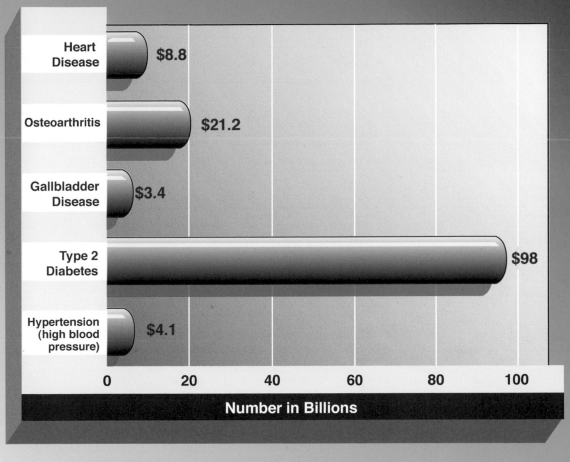

Economic Impact of Obesity-Related Conditions to Society and the Health-Care Industry

Condition	Amount
Heart Disease	$8.8
Osteoarthritis	$21.2
Gallbladder Disease	$3.4
Type 2 Diabetes	$98
Hypertension (high blood pressure)	$4.1

Number in Billions

Source: ObesityinAmerica.org, "Economic Impact of Obesity," www.obesityinamerica.org.

It is Combs' job to set the state's standards for the school breakfast and lunch program. She has exceeded the federal guidelines and instituted rules for Texas schools that eliminate all "competitive foods"—those that compete with healthy choices offered in school breakfast and lunch programs. She touts the economic benefits of this for the state, explaining that if there was 100 percent participation in the school lunch program, Texas would increase its federal share of school nutrition funds by $562 million

Children of poor migrant workers eat a nutritious meal at school.

statewide. Her office also provides training on how to fundraise for revenues that may be lost when competitive foods aren't sold at school.

Combs has talked with Kraft, Cadbury Schweppes, Nestle, Coke and other "agribusiness" executives in an effort to persuade them to offer healthier fare for students. She tells them the public wants smaller portion sizes and fewer calories and says that "everybody is offering healthier," in part, because of concerns about liability.

There is no doubt that the availability of healthy choices encourages healthy lifestyles. Dr. Risa Lavizzo-Mourey, president and CEO of The Robert Wood Johnson Foundation perhaps sums it up best: "Obesity rates are highest in communities afflicted by poverty. Families in these communities simply don't have the same opportunities to make healthy choices as families in other neighborhoods. They don't have grocery stores that stock affordable fresh fruits and vegetables. There aren't enough safe places for kids to play or programs that teach kids physical activity. We must remove these barriers. We want to encourage legislators to be visible, vocal champions of policies that promote nutrition and physical activity."

FIVE

Childhood Obesity Is a National Epidemic

Charles W. Schmidt

In the following selection Charles W. Schmidt argues that childhood obesity is a growing problem in the United States. Although experts say that it is difficult to point to any definite cause for obesity, Schmidt writes, sedentary lifestyles, sprawling urban environments, and growing portion sizes are just a few probable reasons. It is also possible that genetics predisposes some children to obesity, as indicated by some family studies. However, Schmidt points out that many researchers agree that most obese children are overweight as a result of eating high-calorie foods and not doing enough physical activities. Obese children face a number of health and psychological problems, such as diabetes, sleep apnea, heart disease, and depression. In order to combat obesity, programs have been developed across the country to educate children about nutrition and foster an interest in physical activity. Schmidt is the winner of the 2002 National Association of Science Writer's Science-in-Society Journalism Award. He has written for publications such as *New Scientist*, *Journal of the National Cancer Institute*, and *Child Magazine*.

Charles W. Schmidt, "Obesity: A Weighty Issue for Children," *Environmental Health Perspectives*, vol. 111, October 2003. Reproduced by permission.

O h, to be a child in America: Morning cartoons with a breakfast of sugar-coated cereal, hours on the sofa munching chips and playing video games, matinee movies enjoyed with mega-sized servings of soda and popcorn, frozen dinners followed by more hours surfing computer chat rooms, and finally bed. In all, this combination of inactivity and gluttonous feeding, which is shared by millions of American children, fuels one of the country's most alarming pediatric problems: obesity.

According to *America's Children: Key National Indicators of Well-Being 2003*, issued in July 2003 by the Federal Interagency Forum on Child and Family Statistics, the number of overweight and obese children in the United States has more than doubled in the last two decades. . . .

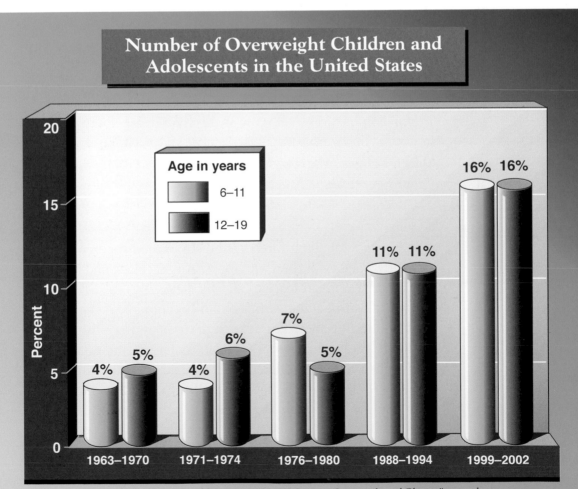

Number of Overweight Children and Adolescents in the United States

Source: Centers for Disease Control and Prevention, "NCHS Data on Overweight and Obesity," www.cdc.gov.

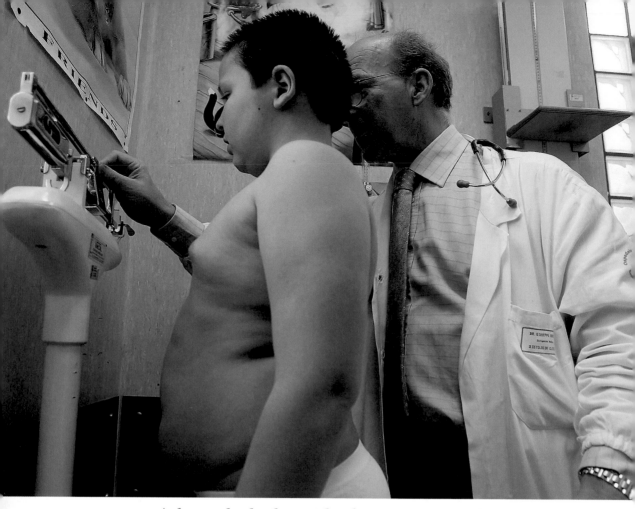

A doctor checks the weight of a young patient who is just one of many overweight American youths.

Today, 15% of all children aged 6–18 exceed the upper range of healthy weights for their age groups. Among black and Hispanic children, the number leaps to an average of 26%.

Obesity can be a dangerous childhood hazard. According to Stephen Daniels, a professor of pediatrics and environmental health at Children's Hospital Medical Center in Cincinnati, many overweight and obese children suffer a range of debilitating health problems such as type 2 diabetes mellitus (which has increased more than 10-fold in children since 1982), sleep apnea, hypertension, and cardiovascular disease, in addition to low self-esteem and depression. Data published in the August 2003 issue of *Archives* of *Pediatrics & Adolescent Medicine* by the American Academy of Pediatrics (AAP) Center for Child Health Research further indicate that nearly 1 million obese U.S. children suffer from a condition called metabolic syndrome. This syndrome, which makes children unusually prone to type 2 diabetes and premature heart disease, is characterized by the presence of at least five criteria: excessive abdominal fat, high blood pressure, high triglyceride levels in blood, low levels of "good" HDL cholesterol, and high blood sugar. . . .

In the long run, says Daniels, obese children are much more likely to become obese adults, and "we are finding that childhood risk factors can be linked to the incidence of adult disease." Many of obesity's associated health problems—diabetes in particular— also become more difficult to manage in older patients. . . .

Researchers who try to pinpoint the specific causes of obesity or quantify the proportional contribution of causes to the obesity epidemic face a tough challenge. It is nearly impossible to definitively link assumed risk factors with the growth of obesity in the population. Researchers can say, for instance, that obesity rates have risen along with suburban sprawl, video games, and super-sized fast-food portions, but they can't say that sprawl, video games, or fast food cause obesity. In general, children become obese for highly individualized reasons. A child who spends hours per day watching television but eats sparingly, for instance, might well still be underweight for his age. In population terms, the epidemic appears to be the result of many interrelated factors, each exacerbating the obesity-promoting effects of the others. . . .

The Effect of the Environment on Activity Levels
The CDC [Centers for Disease Control and Prevention] National Health and Nutrition Examination Survey, a key source of U.S. body weight data, provides no contextual information about physical environments in which obese Americans live, and even fewer data connecting walking or bicycling with health indicators and demographics, [researcher Phil] Bors says.

But some links between activity and the built environment have been established. "Three elements of the built environment that really seem to influence activity levels are perceptions of safety, good lighting, and the availability of sidewalks," says Barbara Ainsworth, who chairs the Department of Exercise and Nutritional Sciences at San Diego State University. In most cases, however, these relationships pertain to adults. It's hard to extrapolate these results to children, says Ainsworth, and the data on children are very rare.

Susan Handy, an associate professor of environmental science and policy at the University of California, Davis, confirmed in the August 2002 supplement to the *American Journal of Preventive*

A young overweight woman takes a moment to cope with her emotions. Obesity can lead to depression and loss of self-esteem.

Health that walkers and cyclists tend to be influenced in their travel decisions by neighborhood factors such as safety, comfort, and aesthetics, whereas drivers typically are not. Urban planning studies such as Handy's show that people are more likely to walk and bicycle in traditional communities populated by nearby shops and services. Those who live in more modern, "auto-dependent" communities are more likely to drive.

Ross Brownson, an epidemiologist at St. Louis University, published evidence in the December 2001 *American Journal of Public Health* showing that people's activity levels increased when they lived close to walking trails, swimming pools, and gyms. Similarly, in one study that did pertain specifically to children, published in *Health Psychology* in September 1993, [psychology professor James] Sallis found that activity levels among 4-year-old children correlated highly with the amount of time they spent outdoors and their access to recreational areas such as playgrounds, parks, and yards. . . .

Fast Food and Nutrition

If the built environment's role in childhood obesity seems complicated, dietary factors in relation to the epidemic are no less so. Nearly every aspect of the dietary contribution is debated, including the role of fats in the diet and the fundamental issue of daily caloric intake. Some scientists lay the blame for obesity squarely on declining activity, insisting that caloric intake has remained stable over time, while others, such as Barbara Rolls, Guthrie Chair in the Department of Nutritional Sciences at The Pennsylvania State University, say it has not. . . .

Rolls believes the population's intake of calories is probably rising. At a minimum, the energy equation between caloric intake and expenditure is, she says, "out of whack." Says Rolls, "We are eating more calories than we need and also exercising less. So, the equation is unbalanced on both sides, which makes it really bad."

A key issue is the body's exquisite sensitivity to fluctuations in the energy balance. A positive energy balance—or extra caloric intake—of just 120 calories per day, equal to about one serving of soda, could produce a 50-kilogram (110-pound) increase in body weight over 10 years. In the 17 February 2001 issue of *The Lancet*, [Harvard researcher David S.] Ludwig and colleagues reported that each additional daily serving of soda increases the risk of childhood obesity by 60%, after controlling for exercise and diet.

Rolls, an expert on the effects of portion size on intake, says that it has become much easier for children and adults alike to get high calorie loads quickly. The real culprits, she says, are energy-dense foods with low fiber content—a dietary universe that includes most of the fast food and processed snacks on the market today. A child who eats a typical fast-food hamburger, fries, and soft drink can consume over 1,200 calories in a single meal, more than half the daily caloric requirement. This tasty meal, which plays to a primordial love of salt, sugar, and fat, is also cheap, which helps to explain why obesity rates are particularly high at the lower end of the socioeconomic spectrum.

Ludwig suggests that one reason people overindulge in these foods is because they have a high glycemic index, meaning they produce a rapid increase in blood sugar. According to Ludwig, the surge in blood glucose and insulin produced by such foods soon crashes and stimulates hunger within a short period. Low-glycemic-index foods such as legumes, fruits, and vegetables, on the other hand, release nutrients more slowly, which leads to less erratic eating habits. Most low-nutritional-quality snacks and soft drinks have a high glycemic index, and they also are made from cheap ingredients such as sugar and potatoes, and thus are profitable, Ludwig says. "This is why they are pushed so aggressively by food companies, who spend billions a year marketing them to kids," he adds.

Increasing Portion Sizes

According to Rolls's research, portion size also has a significant effect on consumption. In her report in the March/April 2003 issue of *Nutrition Today*, she cited data indicating that portions in restaurants, grocery products, and even cookbooks have steadily gotten larger since the 1970s, to the extent that they are now

Checking her calorie guide, this young woman is learning to eat appropriately.

sharply dissociated from the serving sizes recommended by the U.S. Department of Agriculture Food Guide Pyramid. In general, she says, the larger the portion, the more people eat.

This appears to be a learned rather than innate behavior. Rolls found that toddlers below the age of 3 self-regulate their food intake and stop eating when full, regardless of how much they are served. As children get older, they adapt to environmental cues urging them to "clean their plate." Eventually, Rolls's research shows, portion size becomes a major determinant of food consumption.

Meanwhile, time-strapped citizens are eating out more than ever, even as portions served in restaurants, movie theaters, and coffee shops have become enormous. This is the era of "huge food," Rolls says: consumers are surrounded by muffins that weigh half a pound, 2-pound bowls of pasta, 1-pound steaks, and "medium" popcorn servings that contain 16 cups and up to 1,000 calories. . . .

But do large portions cause obesity? As is often the case with environmental epidemiology, proving causality is next to impossible, Rolls says. "[Nonetheless], a body of suggestive evidence can be very persuasive," she adds. "So, for example, on portion size I would say the weight of the evidence suggests we need to do some-

Wayne Stroot. Copyright © 2002 by *The Hastings Tribune*. Reproduced by permission.

thing about large portions [even without conducting] a study to see if we can directly fatten people up by serving them large portions!" . . .

The Role of Genetics

One of obesity's more intriguing features is the variability with which it is expressed among different ethnicities and nationalities. For instance, Scandinavian obesity rates are especially low relative to the rest of the world. And South Pacific Islanders, in addition to indigenous populations in Latin America, have rates that are exorbitantly high. Could genetics play a role? Claude Bouchard, executive director of the Pennington Biomedical Research Center in Baton Rouge, Louisiana, and an expert on the genetics of obesity, says it's possible that some populations may be genetically more predisposed to obesity than others, but there is "absolutely no scientific evidence to support the contention."

The general consensus among experts is that genetic factors do modulate environmental risks for obesity. According to Claudio Maffeis, a professor of pediatrics at the University of Verona in Italy, evidence from twin, adoption, and family studies strongly suggests that biological relatives exhibit similarities in the maintenance of body weight. Some children seem to be genetically immune to the effects of overeating. Others continue to gain weight no matter how hard they try to shed the extra pounds.

But these extremes are a genetic minority, Bouchard says. Among most populations, the genetic contributions are graded— some children are more prone toward obesity, others less. The obesity outcome, he explains, becomes manifest only under the right environmental or lifestyle conditions. . . .

Raising Awareness About Obesity

Around the country, a range of public health programs are working to increase education about obesity and promote efforts to slow its growth. Project SPARK, coordinated by Sallis and [the national program he heads,] Active Living Research, has developed

The boy in the photograph seems to take after his father in terms of being overweight, but scientists say most weight problems are not genetic.

age-specific school-based approaches that seek to build motor coordination among children from prekindergarten through middle school to bolster self-esteem and interest in physical activity. The program for younger children also emphasizes building children's social skills in a physical education environment, for example by teaching them to share equipment and cooperate.

"We need programs in schools that help kids learn how to make healthful choices in physical activity and nutrition," Sallis says. "Furthermore, there is no excuse for selling and serving foods of limited nutritional value in schools, but it is done everywhere. Financial support for school food services needs to be increased so they can afford to provide healthful foods to kids."

Hill adds that the first step for clinicians should be to shift the emphasis away from weight loss to a cessation of weight gain. "Small changes—eating a bit less, walking a bit more—can stop weight gain and produce an enormous public health benefit," he says. "Our priorities are in the wrong place right now. We're focusing on obese people and trying to make them lean. We need to focus all our efforts on stopping weight gain."

SIX

The Fast-Food Industry Contributes to Obesity

Amanda Spake and Mary Brophy Marcus

In the past few decades Americans have begun to consume an increasing number of calories from fast-food meals and processed snacks, which typically contain high percentages of saturated fats and sugar. This food is sold nearly everywhere—from gas stations and vending machines to food courts in shopping malls. In the following viewpoint journalists Amanda Spake and Mary Brophy Marcus argue that this increased availability of fast food is playing a large role in the escalating numbers of Americans who suffer from obesity. In addition, the trend of "supersizing" menu items in fast-food establishments is leading Americans to consume more food than ever before. For example, whereas a typical order of movie popcorn in the 1950s was about three cups, the average size is now sixteen cups, containing at least nine hundred calories. Moreover, the authors contend, the increased advertising of candy, soft drinks, and fast food also contributes to the overconsumption of these items. Spake and Marcus are writers for U.S. *News & World Report*.

Pretty, dark-haired Katie Young has been successful at most things. She's a nearly straight-A student, a big hitter on her softball team, and a good dancer. But like so many Americans—kids and adults alike—the New Orleans 10-year-old struggles with one thing: keeping her weight under control.

When Katie started day camp in June, she discovered a snack bar where she could buy pizza, hot dogs, candy, ice cream, chips,

This overweight teen is part of a generation whose biggest health issue may be obesity.

Supersized Servings

Burger King Hamburger	1954 2.8 oz. 202 calories	2004 4.3 oz. 310 calories
McDonald's French Fries	1955 2.4 oz. 210 calories	2004 7 oz. 610 calories
Hershey's Chocolate Bar	1900 2 oz. 297 calories	2004 7 oz. 1000 calories
Coca-Cola Soft Drink	1916 6.5 fluid oz. 79 calories	2004 16 fluid oz. 194 calories
Movie Popcorn	1950s 3 cups 174 calories	2004 21 cups (buttered) 1,700 calories

Source: Cathy Newman, *National Geographic*, August 2004.

soft drinks, and more. "Katie went nuts," says her mother, Judy Young. In the first two weeks of camp, Katie stole nearly $40 from her mother's purse for snack foods. "I bought a lot of pizza," Katie says. "It's good, of course, because it's from Pizza Hut. And I bought candy and everything. I didn't feel good seeing the other kids eat those things. I wanted them too."

Of course she did. Katie was acting on a basic driving force of human biology: Eat whenever food is available and eat as much of it as possible. Throughout most of human history, food was scarce, and getting ahold of it required a great deal of physical energy. Those who ate as many calories as they could were protected against famine and had the energy to reproduce. "As a result, humans are hard-wired to prefer rich diets, high in fat, sugar, and variety," says Kelly Brownell, director of the Yale Center for Eating and Weight Disorders. The problem today, Brownell adds, is that there's "a complete mismatch" between biology and the environment. Or as University of Colorado nutrition researcher James Hill puts it, "Our physiology tells us to eat whenever food is available. And now, food is always available."

National girth. America has become a fat nation. More than 61 percent of adults are overweight, and 27 percent of them—50 million people—are obese, according to a U.S. surgeon general's report released last December [2001]. In the next decade, weight-related illnesses threaten to overwhelm the healthcare system. New evidence from the Framingham Heart Study shows that obesity doubles the risk of heart failure in women. A man with 22 extra pounds has a 75 percent greater chance of having a heart attack than one at healthy weight. Gaining just 11 to 18 pounds doubles the risk of developing Type II diabetes—an illness that has increased by nearly 50 percent in only the past decade.

Too Much Food

Weight is also taking a heavy toll on the nation's children. The percentage of 6- to 11-year-olds who are overweight has nearly doubled in two decades, and for adolescents the percentage has tripled. Pediatricians are treating conditions rarely before diagnosed in young people. In a recent study of 813 overweight Louisiana schoolchildren, for example, 58 percent had at least one heart-disease risk factor, such as high blood pressure, cholesterol, or insulin levels. Four percent of adolescents now have "adult onset" (or Type II) diabetes, and in some clinics teens represent half of all new cases.

Obesity has been linked to everything from the decline of the family dinner to the popularity of computers and video games to supersize portions of fast food. But it all comes down to a simple calculation, says Colorado's Hill: "The primary reason America is fat is that we eat too much compared to our activity level."

Over the past 50 years, as technology has reduced movement in daily life, the American diet has also changed, paralleling a revolution in food production. "The energy intensity of the human diet is going up," says Barry Popkin, a professor of nutrition at the University of North Carolina–Chapel Hill [UNC]. Human beings are eating more calories per bite than their ancestors ate. "The most common changes," Popkin explains, "are the added sugar in processed food and the added fat."

Without question the food industry has delivered something unique in human history: a dependable, low-cost food supply. "But now, food is so overproduced in the U.S. that there are 3,800 calories per person per day, and we only need about half of that," says Marion Nestle, chair of the Department of Nutrition and Food Studies at New York University [NYU]. Judy Putnam, who studies food and nutritional patterns for the U.S. Department of Agriculture [USDA], agrees. USDA food-supply data show a 500-calorie-per-person daily increase between 1984 and 2000. Similarly, the USDA's dietary intake surveys show a 236-calorie-per-person-per-day increase between 1987 and 1995. Even that smaller estimate translates into an average 24-pound weight gain per person every year. Putnam figures that about 39 percent of the increase comes from refined grains, 32 percent from added fats, and 24 percent from more sugar.

Hard to believe, but Americans consume the equivalent of 20 to 33 teaspoons of sugar per person per day. About 30 percent of it is in soft drinks, but sugar is also the No. 1 additive. It is found in a variety of foods, says Putnam: "It turns up in some unlikely places, such as pizza, bread, hot dogs, soup, crackers, spaghetti sauce, lunchmeat, canned vegetables, fruit drinks, flavored yogurt, ketchup, salad dressing, and mayonnaise."

Greater use of prepared foods may have increased calories, but so has another major cultural change: eating out. Restaurant meals generally contain more fat, including more saturated fat, less fiber, more cholesterol, and more calories than homemade meals. In 1977–78, Americans ate about 19 percent of their total calories out. By 1995, they were eating 34 percent of their calories away from home. "The size of this increase is enormous," says UNC's Popkin, who analyzes the USDA's dietary surveys. "There has been a more than doubling of the calories consumed at restaurants and fast-food establishments over the past two decades."

Supersizing Adds Mega-calories

That's in part because when people do eat out, they eat more—one result of the supersizing trend that's sweeping the market. "The food is the least of the cost of a food product. Labor, packaging, marketing cost more," says NYU's Nestle. "So, it's very profitable to make larger portions." When McDonald's opened, its original burger, fries, and 12-ounce Coke provided 590 calories. Today, a supersize Extra Value Meal with a Quarter Pounder With Cheese, supersize fries, and a supersize drink is 1,550 calories. An order of movie theater popcorn was about 3 cups in 1957. Now, the typical medium theater popcorn is 16 cups and 900 calories.

The supersizing of meal portions, especially at popular fast-food restaurants like McDonald's, has been linked to America's obesity problems.

A 7-Eleven 64-ounce Double Gulp has nearly 800 calories, 10 times as many as the original 6.5-ounce bottles of Coca-Cola.

According to the Center for Science in the Public Interest, many fast-food chains encourage customers to order "supersize" items, pointing out that they get more value for their dollar. At the Cinnabon pastry chain, for example, a 3-ounce Minibon costs about $2, but for only about 50 cents more the customer can feast on an 8-ounce Cinnabon. What's not advertised, however, is the fact that this bargain raises caloric intake from 300 to 670. The trend in "value marketing" also means that chain restaurants combine foods into a meal that often costs less than buying each item separately. For example, the Center for Science in the Public Interest [CSPI] reports that at McDonald's, a Quarter Pounder With Cheese, medium fries, and medium soft drink purchased separately cost an average of $5.03. But an Extra Value Meal with the same items costs just $3.74. There is also the option of mak-

Young boys exercise in a weight-loss program in Missouri. The number of overweight adolescents in the United States has tripled since 1980.

ing the "value" meal even larger. At Wendy's, the Classic Double With Cheese Old-Fashioned Combo Meal costs $4.89 and has 1,360 calories. For only 39 cents more, one can "biggie size" the meal and eat 1,540 calories.

And when that supersize portion is served to your table or car window, says Nestle, "there is something about our psychology that makes us eat more if it's put in front of us." Pennsylvania State University nutrition professor Barbara Rolls demonstrated precisely this phenomenon. In her study, lean young men, known to regulate food intake well, were given different portions of macaroni and cheese for lunch on different days. When served 16 ounces, they ate 10, but when given the 25-ounce "jumbo lunch," they ate 15 ounces, 50 percent more than what had satisfied them previously.

Snacking All Day Long

Not only are Americans eating more at meals, they're eating more meals. Snacking has increased so much, says UNC's Popkin, "that children eat about five meals now and adults eat 4½. A quarter of children's calories now come from snacks, and the typical snack is no longer an apple. Snacks are often potato chips or tortilla chips." Two decades ago, snacks made up only 11.3 percent of the diet. By 1996, that figure was 17.7 percent. Consumption of salty snack foods has doubled in the past 20 years, according to a UNC study.

Eating opportunities are endless because food is sold almost everywhere. "Just go back 20 years," says Yale's Brownell. "You never used to find more than a candy counter in a drugstore. Now there are aisles and aisles of food. If you see a gas station that does not have a food store attached, people are afraid to use it. There are food courts in shopping malls. And in the schools, there are vending machines and soft-drink machines—and they aren't selling carrot juice."

In fact, most of these eating venues are selling the same foods—candy, soft drinks, salty snacks, pastries, ice cream, cookies, nachos, pizza, hot dogs, cheeseburgers, and other fried foods. These are some of the food companies' most profitable items, and they received the lion's share of the $11 billion the industry spent on advertising in 1997. Indeed, food companies are the second-largest advertisers in the U.S. economy, just behind automobiles. About $1.54 billion of the total went toward advertising prepared, processed, and convenience foods. Fast-food and food-service companies spent an additional $3.1 billion. In comparison with these ad dollars, the USDA's nutrition education budget is roughly $333 million, about the same as the advertising budget for coffee, tea, and cocoa.

There seems to be little connection between people's understanding of food availability and eating behavior and an awareness of their expanding waistlines. In an American Institute for Cancer Research survey in 2000, more than 3 in 4 of those polled said that the kind of food they ate was more important in maintaining or losing weight than the amount of food. Americans' false hope that calories don't count may explain a general ignorance about how much people are actually eating. In that same survey, 62 percent said that compared to 10 years ago restaurant portions are the same size or smaller. Few said they measured out food portions when they eat, nor could most correctly estimate a "serving" of pasta based on the USDA's portion guidelines. Not surprisingly, a sizable majority said they were overweight. Likewise, in a Harvard University survey released in May 2002, more than half of those surveyed said they were overweight. But 78 percent did not think their weight was a problem. Though the vast majority regarded cancer, AIDS, and heart disease as serious health problems, only a third thought obesity was.

Fast Foods at School

Scientists are not sure whether it's the sedentary nature of television viewing, food consumption in front of the TV, food adver-

Sugary drinks can be found just about everywhere, including in schools like this one.

tising—or all of them—that promote obesity. "But more things are beginning to point toward food consumption," says William Dietz, director of Nutrition and Physical Activity at the federal Centers for Disease Control and Prevention [CDC]. TV prompts kids to eat, says Dietz. A study in last week's [August 2002] *Lancet* shows that U.S. children see about 10 food commercials during every hour of TV they watch. In the Young household now, Katie must "buy" her TV time with 30-minute coupons her mother issues as payment for finishing her homework in after-school care.

In two years, Katie will go to middle school, and "she's going to have more access to food outside of my control," her mother says. Indeed, CDC studies show that 73.9 percent of middle and junior high schools have either vending machines or snack bars where

Students dine on soft drinks and nachos at a school cafeteria. Many states are considering banning junk foods from schools.

high-calorie foods and soft drinks are sold, and 98.2 percent of senior high schools do. More than 23 percent of schools allow companies to advertise candy, fast foods, or soft drinks through distribution of coupons for free or reduced-cost foods. More than 20 percent of schools serve brand-name fast foods, often as part of the USDA-funded National School Lunch Program. The USDA's Stanley Garnett, director of Child Nutrition Programs, says the agency cannot legally restrict the use of fast foods as long as "nutritional standards averaged over a week are met" in the USDA-funded programs.

About 50 percent of school districts have "pouring rights" contracts that allow soft drink companies to sell beverages in the districts' schools; some schools have individual contracts instead. Schools and districts receive a percentage of sales. At 37 percent of schools, payments are tied directly to a quota of drink sales. One Colorado administrator wrote a memo suggesting that in order to sell enough soft drinks, faculty and staff "allow students to purchase and consume vended products throughout the day."

School administrators say they have to sign these agreements to have money to provide students with computers, sports teams, and more. Even Education Secretary Roderick Paige negotiated a $5 million exclusive contract with Coca-Cola in 2000 when he headed the Houston school district.

It should not be surprising, then, that the USDA reports 56 percent to 85 percent of children drink sodas every day. Adolescent boys drink, on average, three sugared soft drinks a day; even toddlers drink 7 ounces. Soft drinks have replaced milk in many youngsters' diets.

Soft drinks are increasingly under attack for their possible contribution to childhood obesity. David Ludwig, director of the Obesity Program at Children's Hospital Boston, says his research shows that "for every additional serving of soft drinks a day, a child's risk of becoming obese increases by 60 percent." Ludwig's soft drink study also suggests that calories from sugar-sweetened drinks do not seem to be as filling as calories from other foods.

Soon after Ludwig's results hit the media, studies paid for by the National Soft Drink Association [NSDA], used government data to show that soft drinks do not cause pediatric obesity. "If you go through all the scientific evidence, you see there is no link between sugar consumption or soft-drink consumption and obesity," says Sean McBride of the NSDA. "Any food or beverage that contains calories can contribute to weight gain, but singling out any one factor for a very complex problem is misguided." This debate is only beginning: New data from Denmark indicate that overweight adults who consumed the equivalent of about two to four 20-ounce nondiet soft drinks per day for 10 weeks gained weight and body fat and their blood pressure increased, compared with a control group drinking artificially sweetened beverages.

School Rules

Efforts are underway in at least 10 states to limit the sale of soft drinks and snack foods in schools, and some states have already imposed restrictions. Under USDA regulations, foods of "minimal nutritional value," such as soft drinks, are not to be sold where National School Lunch and Breakfast meals are served and eaten. To get around the rule, some schools put vending machines and snack bars outside, but near, school cafeterias.

But last spring [2002], the Texas Education Agency issued a directive to districts that beginning this fall [2002] foods of minimal nutritional value will not be sold in cafeterias, hallways, or common areas—at all. California legislators passed a bill scheduled to take effect in 2004 that sets nutritional standards for food sold in elementary schools and effectively bans sodas, high-fat foods, and fruit drinks with less than 50 percent juice or with added sugar. A bill to phase out soft-drink sales in all schools failed, however. The food industry opposed the bill, but so did the California Teachers Association, which argued that schools would be deprived of needed cash. "For society to fund education by promoting consumption of such unhealthy products," says Boston's Ludwig, "is among the worst kinds of investments we can make." . . .

To make the public more calorie-conscious when dining out, health advocates want chain and fast-food restaurants to list the calorie content of their meals prominently on menus and food wrappers. "It wouldn't cost anything," says Michael Jacobson, director of CSPI, who first proposed this idea, "but it could have a major effect on food choices."

These and other obesity-prevention ideas could slim our collective paunch. But for some people, like Judy Young, the benefits won't come soon enough. "I've been on the liquid diet, fen-phen, Redux. I tried Atkins and the Zone," she says. Nothing lasted. This fall, Young plans to undergo gastric bypass surgery, a procedure in which the stomach is sectioned off and a small pouch is created, reducing the amount of food one can eat. Gastric bypass is only recommended for people who are 100 pounds or more overweight. Weight loss is rapid, but high rates of complications are associated with the surgery, and as many as 2 in 100 patients die from it.

Young knows these risks. She says she has weighed them again and again. "If I don't do it," she says, "I don't think I will live to see Katie grow up."

SEVEN

The Fast-Food Industry Is Not Responsible for Obesity Rates

Todd G. Buchholz

The fast-food industry has been blamed for the growing numbers of overweight people in the United States and has been the target of a variety of criticisms from nutritionists, environmentalists, and animal rights activists. In the following viewpoint Todd G. Buchholz argues that although Americans consume more calories and are less physically active than in previous decades, the fast-food industry is not to blame. Many of the extra calories people consume come from snacks bought at grocery stores—a fact that the obesity lawsuits against fast-food establishments fail to recognize. While it is possible to become overweight by eating fast food, Buchholz writes, many franchises offer customers information regarding the nutritional value of menu items and provide a number of healthy alternatives. People must make a personal choice about whether they want to eat a greasy cheeseburger at a fast-food restaurant or a salad at home, he contends. If customers choose to ignore the healthy items in favor of the more fattening ones, he argues, they do not have a right to blame fast-food restaurants for their choices. Buchholz is the cofounder and managing director of Enso Capital Management. He has also served as a White House economic adviser and is the author of *New Ideas from Dead Economists* and *Market Shock: 9 Economic and Social Upheavals That Will Shake Our Financial Future*.

Todd G. Buchholz, "Are Fast-Food Establishments Making Americans Fat?" *Journal of Controversial Medical Claims*, vol. 10, November 2003, pp. 1–10. Reprinted by permission of Aspen Publishers.

Fast-food restaurants have exploded in popularity since World War II. More cars, more suburbs, and more roads have made roadside eating more convenient. During the 1950s, drive-through and drive-in burger, ice cream, and pizza joints catered to a mobile population. . . .

And yet despite the popularity of such fast-food firms as McDonald's, Wendy's, Burger King, Pizza Hut, Taco Bell, Subway, etc.—at which American consumers voluntarily spend over $100 billion annually—it has become quite fashionable to denounce these restaurants for a variety of reasons. "They make people fat." "They hypnotize the kids." "They bribe the kids with toys." "They destroy our taste for more sophisticated foods." These condemnations often come from highbrow sources claiming that customers of fast food are too ignorant or too blinded to understand what they are putting in their own mouths. . . .

With the fury directed at fast-food firms, it is no surprise that tort lawyers have jumped into the fray. Tort lawyers around the

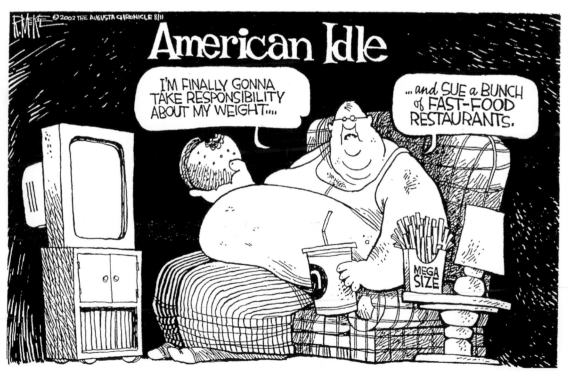

Rick McKee. Copyright © 2005 by *The Augusta Chonicle* 8/11. Reproduced by permission.

country settled the $246 billion tobacco case in 1998. Those who have not retired on their stake from that settlement are wondering whether fast food could be the "next tobacco," along with HMOs [health maintenance organizations] and lead paint. After all, the Surgeon General estimates that obesity creates about $117 billion in annual healthcare costs.

There are differences, of course. No one, so far, has shown that cheeseburgers are chemically addictive. Furthermore, most fast-food restaurants freely distribute their nutritional content and offer a variety of meals, some high in fat, some not. Nor is it clear that the average fast-food meal is significantly less nutritious than the average restaurant meal, or even the average home meal. The iconic 1943 Norman Rockwell Thanksgiving painting ("Freedom from Want") highlights a plump turkey, which is high in protein. But surely the proud hostess has also prepared gravy, stuffing, and a rich pie for dessert, which though undoubtedly tasty, would not win a round of applause from nutritionists. . . .

Americans Consume More Calories Now than Ever Before

Should we chiefly blame fast-food firms for BMIs[1] over 25? According to the caricature described by lawyers suing fast-food companies, poor, ill-educated people are duped by duplicitous fast-food franchises into biting into greasy hamburgers and french fries. The data tell us that this theory is wrong. If the "blame fast food" hypothesis were right, we would see a faster pace of BMI growth among poorly educated people, who might not be able to read or understand nutritional labels. In fact, college-educated, not poorly educated people accounted for the most rapid growth in BMI scores between the 1970s and the 1990s—though poorly educated people still have a higher overall incidence of obesity. The percentage of obese college-educated women nearly tripled between the early 1970s and the early 1990s. In comparison, the proportion of obese women without high school degrees rose by only 58

1. The BMI, or Body Mass Index, is a ratio of height to weight used to calculate whether a person is obese or overweight. A score of 20–25 is considered normal range.

percent. Among men, the results were similar. Obesity among those without high school degrees climbed by about 53 percent. But obesity among college graduates jumped by 163 percent. If the "blame fast food" hypothesis made sense, these data would be flipped upside down.

Of course, we cannot deny that people are eating more and getting bigger. But that does not prove that fast-food franchises are the culprit. On average, Americans are eating about 200 calories more each day than they did in the 1970s. An additional 200 calories can be guzzled in a glass of milk, a soda, or gobbled in a bowl of cereal, for example. Fast-food critics eagerly pounce and allege that the additional calories come from super-sized meals of pizza, burgers, or burritos. It is true that between the 1970s and the 1990s, daily fast-food intake grew from an average of 60 calories to 200 calories. But simply quoting that data misleads. Though Americans have been consuming somewhat more fast food at mealtime, they have reduced their home consumption at mealtime. Americans have cut back their home meals by about 228 calories for men and 177 for women, offsetting the rise in fast food calories.

In total, mealtime calories have not budged much, and mealtimes are when consumers generally visit fast-food restaurants. So where are the 200 additional calories coming from? The U.S. Department of Agriculture [USDA] has compiled the "Continuing Survey of Food Intakes by Individuals," which collects information on where a food was purchased, how it was prepared, and where it was eaten, in addition to demographic information, such as race, income, age, and sex. The Survey shows us that Americans are not eating bigger breakfasts, lunches, or dinners. But they are noshing and nibbling like never before. . . .

Where do Americans eat their between-meal calories? Mostly at home. Kitchen cabinets can be deadly to diets. And in a fairly recent development, supermarket shoppers are pulling goodies off of store shelves and ripping into them at the stores before they can even drive home. Consumers eat two to three times more goodies inside stores than at fast-food restaurants.

Why are people eating more and growing larger? For one thing, food is cheaper. From a historical point of view that is a very good

your favorite fruits.

New!
Fresh Fruit
Bowl & Cup

Excellent source of Vitamin A & C

Young Wendy's patrons choose a healthier alternative to burgers and fries. Most fast-food chains now offer side dishes such as fresh fruit (inset).

thing. A smaller portion of today's family budget goes to food than at anytime during the twentieth century. In 1929, families spent 23.5 percent of their incomes on food. In 1961, they spent 17 percent. By 2001, American families spent just 10 percent of their incomes on food. The lower relative cost of food made it easier, of course, for people to consume more. . . .

Despite the attraction of restaurant eating and the proliferation of sit-down chain restaurants such as the Olive Garden, TGI Friday's, P.F. Chang's, etc., Americans still consume about two thirds of their calories at home. Critics of fast food spend little time comparing fast-food meals to meals eaten at home, at schools, or at sit-down restaurants.

Sedentary Jobs Provide Fewer Chances to Burn Calories

The nature of the American workplace may also be contributing to higher caloric intake. Whether people dine while sitting down at a table or while standing at a fast-food counter, at the workplace they are literally sitting down on the job more than they did during prior eras. More sedentary desk jobs probably contribute to wider bottoms. Consider two middle-income jobs, one in 1953 and one in 2003. In 1953, a dockworker lifts 50 boxes off of a mini-crane and places it on a hand truck, which the dockworker pulls to a warehouse. In 2003, a person earning a similar income would be sitting in front of a computer, inputting data, and matching orders with deliveries. . . .

A person telecommuting from home may be sitting even closer to the refrigerator or cupboard. In 1970, the term "telecommuting" did not even exist. By 2000, however, with advances in computers and remote access technology, approximately 12 percent of the workforce worked from home at least part of the week. This figure does not include over 25 million home-based businesses. Casual observation implies that many telecommuters take breaks from their homework at coffee shops and other sellers of baked goods. . . .

Fast-Food May Be Less Fattening than Some Home-Cooked Meals

Very few defenders of fast food would tell moms and dads to throw out the home-cooked meal and instead eat 21 meals a week at a fast-food restaurant. But it is a mistake to stereotype fast food as simply a cheeseburger and large fries. Fast-food restaurants have vastly expanded their menus for a variety of reasons, including health concerns and demographic shifts. . . .

In fact, fast-food meals today derive fewer calories from fat than they did in the 1970s. Consumers can customize their fast-food meals, too. Simply by asking for "no mayo," they may cut down fat calories by an enormous proportion. It is worth pointing out that fast-food firms introduced these alternative meals in response to changing consumer tastes, not in reply to dubious lawsuits. During the 1990s, McDonald's and Taco Bell invested millions of dollars trying to develop low-fat, commercially viable selections such as the McLean Deluxe hamburger and Taco Bell's Border Lights. Burger King adopted its "Have It Your Way" slogan several decades ago.

While plaintiffs' lawyers vigorously denounce the nutritional content of fast food, they tend to ignore the nutritional content of alternatives. Home cooking, of course, has a nice ring to it, and it is hard to criticize the idea of a traditional meal cooked by mom or dad. But if we put nostalgia aside for a moment, we can see that the typical American meal of 25 years ago might win taste contests but few prizes from today's nutritionists. Meat loaf, fried chicken, butter-whipped potatoes, and a tall glass of whole milk may have kept us warm on a cold winter evening. But such a diet would surely fail a modern test for healthy living. And let's not even discuss a crusty apple pie or bread pudding for dessert. Yesterday's "comfort" food gives today's dietitians indigestion. No surprise then that today's fast food derives a smaller percentage of calories from fat than a typical home meal from 1977–1978. In fact, even in the 1970s, fast-food meals had almost the same fat/calorie ratio as home cooking at that time. By this measure of fat/calories, fast food in the 1970s looked healthier than restaurant cooking. Therefore, the caricature of fast food as a devilish place for nutrition makes little historical sense. . . .

Schools and Sit-Down Restaurants Do Not Offer Healthier Food

How do fast-food meals compare to schools? Despite the legions of concerned dieticians and PTA leaders, school meals do not look considerably better on the test of fat. While schools provide slightly fewer fat calories, they deliver more saturated fat than fast food, the more dangerous subset of fats. The comparison to sit-down restaurants is similar, with no clear advantage to either fast-food or sit-down restaurants. Of course, fast-food firms have made it easier for patrons to learn about nutritional content than fancier kinds of food outlets. Few patrons of the fabled 21 Club in New York would know that its $26 hamburger is made with rendered duck fat. . . .

In sum, the facts show that obese plaintiffs might just as well walk up to a fast-food counter rather than tuck a napkin under their chins and dine at a chic restaurant or at a school.

Fast-food critics also like to criticize portion sizes. True, fast-food restaurants have been offering super-sized sandwiches, drinks, and french fries. But have these critics been to a movie theater lately, where popcorn containers look like bushel baskets? Or to fancy restaurants featuring all-you-can-eat Sunday buffets? A study in the *Journal of the American Medical Association* cited the "most surprising result [as] the large portion-size increases for food consumed at home—a shift that indicates marked changes in eating behavior in general." People eat bigger portions of hamburgers,

A theater concession worker fills a popcorn order. Movie popcorn servings have grown, in some cases, to bucket-sized servings.

fries, and Mexican food on their own kitchen tables than when they are sitting on a fast-food stool. The study found that "the average home-cooked hamburger now weighs in at about eight ounces, versus perhaps 5.5 ounces in full-service restaurants and a little over seven ounces at fast-food outlets." . . .

Fast Food and Protein per Dollar

There are many measures of nutritional value. In an earlier time, we might simply measure calories per dollar. Because, however, critics accuse fast food of selling "empty" calories (that is, calories comprised of fats and sugars), I have developed a more specific benchmark, namely "cost per gram of protein." Protein is the building block for muscles, and animal protein foods, including meat, poultry, fish, dairy products and eggs, contain the [nine] essential amino acids that cannot be synthesized in the body. Using the ratio of dollar/protein gram seems reasonable and, because it does not include fats and sugars, creates a tougher test for fast food than, for example, dollar/calorie.

Comparing the cost of protein obtained at fast-food restaurants to protein obtained at supermarkets, this study finds that fast-food restaurants provide reasonable value to the consumer, considering the cost of raw materials and the cost of time in preparing meals. In a survey of fast-food chains and supermarkets in five southern California communities (where the fast-food chains and the supermarkets were located within the same towns), I compared the cost of purchasing a "marquee" hamburger, a grilled chicken sandwich, a fish sandwich, a sliced turkey sandwich, and a green salad. The results suggest that in some cases consumers can actually purchase a high protein meal at a fast-food chain for less than the cost of buying the separate groceries at a supermarket and preparing the sandwich themselves. The comparisons understate the cost of supermarket purchases for two principal reasons:

Supermarket prices generally reflect a cost savings for purchasing a larger quantity. You can order one fish fillet from Burger King; it is nearly impossible to buy a single frozen fish fillet in your supermarket.

- Supermarket prices do not reflect the time and cost to the shopper of preparing the meal at home. Nor have I included the extra ingredients such as pickles, relish, onion, mustard, etc. There is little doubt that for a worker earning the average hourly rate (which is $15, according to the Bureau of Labor Statistics) preparing a cooked sandwich would cost far more in materials and time than simply purchasing it from a fast-food restaurant. Even for a minimum wage worker earning $5.15 per hour, a fast-food sandwich is probably much cheaper than spending 30 minutes preparing and grilling a hamburger, fish fillet, or chicken breast. . . .
- In sum, fast food provides in a number of cases competitively priced foods per gram of protein. For people who lack the

time, kitchen space, or ability to purchase from grocery stores and cook at home, fast-food can provide significant benefits. Furthermore, if consumers choose with some level of prudence from the fast-food menus, they can eat fairly nutritious meals. . . .

Nutritional Foods

What has been more fickle than diet recommendations over the years, which continuously spark new fads? In the 1980s and early 1990s, "carbo-loading" was hot, and steaming bowls of pasta shoved roast beef off the dinner table. Today a plate of pasta scares those on the popular, low-carbohydrate Atkins diet, who are instructed to load up their breakfast plates with fried eggs, ham, and bacon while leaving toast off to the side. According to the Atkins Approach, it is fine to bite into a greasy hamburger, but don't dare chew on the bun. . . .

McDonald's CEO Jim Skinner introduces the chain's new food packaging that includes nutritional information aimed at helping consumers make better choices.

U.S. - Big Mac®

Calories	28%	560
Protein	50%	25g
Fat	47%	30g
Carbs	16%	47g
Sodium	42%	1010mg

Surely you might say, there are obvious national standards such as the official US Department of Agriculture's food pyramid. Why not force fast-food firms to serve meals that fit into the pyramid's architecture? The pyramid tells us to eat at least six servings of grain (breads, pasta, etc.) each day, two servings of fruit, and only a little bit of fat or sweets. Sounds reasonable, no? Here is what the controversial head of the Harvard School of Public Health says about the pyramid: "Some people are likely to die from following the USDA pyramid because they will be eliminating healthy fats, such as liquid vegetable oils, that actually reduce the risk of heart disease." Who should Wendy's listen to? The US government or Harvard? Is this a fair choice for a restaurant? . . .

Fast-food chains did not start out by conspiring to sell diabolical menus. Over the past 20 years, homes and fast-food restaurants have pursued lower-fat menus (though homes have admittedly moved more quickly). This would be expected because commercial restaurants would tend to follow the tastes of patrons. Today, nearly every fast-food restaurant offers non-fried poultry and low-fat salads. Further, within 20 seconds of inquiring, each of the fast-food chains mentioned in this study produced nutritional content charts.

Should we expect or demand that fast food lead the march to better menus? How could they? What would they base it on? The US government's nutrition pyramid? The Harvard pyramid? The Atkins diet? Weight Watchers? Oprah's personal plan? Clearly the best avenue is for fast-food firms to provide choices and provide information so that customers can be informed, prudent, and as up-to-date as they would like. . . .

Depending on what you pile on it, a fast-food burger may not enhance your health and it may even hinder your ability to run a marathon—but it is very easy to find out how fatty that burger is. You do not need a tort lawyer by your side to pry open a brochure or to check the thousands of Web sites that will provide nutrition data. Lawsuits against fast-food firms fail to recognize the fact that people choose what and how they want to eat. While it is unlikely that nutritionists will soon announce that super-sized double-cheeseburgers will make you thin, society should not allow the latest fads or the most lucrative lawsuits to govern what we eat for lunch.

EIGHT

Obesity Is a Biological Disease

David Cameron

In the following viewpoint David Cameron describes new advances in the medical understanding of the biology of obesity. In 1994 scientists studying the genomes of obese mice discovered a gene that regulates leptin, a hormone that helps to regulate appetite and feelings of hunger. Mice that do not produce enough leptin have difficulty knowing when to stop eating, Cameron writes. Researchers also found that some obese people do not produce enough leptin and can be treated with injections of the hormone. Further studies show that both obese mice and obese people can become deficient in adiponectin, a hormone secreted by fat cells that helps the body burn fat and sugar. However, although obese mice injected with adiponectin quickly lost their excess weight, injections of the hormone have not helped people to overcome obesity. Cameron notes that researchers are continuing to work to develop drugs that will help people burn calories more quickly and lose weight. Scientists are also working to further their understanding of obesity and how the disease affects people's metabolism and immune systems. Cameron is the media relations manager for the Whitehead Institute for Biomedical Research.

David Cameron, "Fat Chance: The Biology of Obesity," *Paradigm*, Spring 2005, pp. 20–23. Reproduced by permission.

I magine this public-health drama as a film with two parallel plot lines.

Here's the first plot line: The U.S. has a problem, a *big* problem. We're increasingly becoming a nation of overweight—and often downright obese—people. Just look at the numbers. Statistics from 1985 show that less than 10% of the populations of New York and California qualified as being obese. Fast forward to 2001, and that number jumps all the way to 24%.

The second plot line unravels another drama: The onslaught of type 2 diabetes. This disease, afflicting nearly 10% of adults and a rapidly increasing number of children, is the leading cause of blindness and kidney failure, and ranks sixth on the list of killers. And the number of cases is soaring.

You've probably guessed the first plot twist: Both stories star the same villain.

While obesity plays a big role in other diseases ranging from cardiovascular disease to cancer, it tracks particularly well with the epidemic of diabetes. The state of Mississippi offers one telling example. While the rates of obesity there climbed from 10% to over 25% during the 1990s, rates of type 2 diabetes climbed from 6% to over 10%.

In a Supersized nation where Burger King's latest breakfast sandwich weighs in at 730 calories and 47 grams of fat, more and more people have trouble squeezing their stomachs behind the steering wheel as they head over to the drive-through.

But the plot thickens yet again: Advances in medical understanding of the biology of obesity offer hope for a happy ending.

As these twin epidemics explode, so has our knowledge of the key molecules and mechanisms responsible for giving fat a bad name—findings that many pharma companies are now trying to exploit with anti-obesity therapies.

Harvey Lodish, a Founding Whitehead [Institute for Biomedical Research] Member and professor of biology at MIT [Massachusetts Institute of Technology], has pioneered this field. Lodish opened up the field of glucose transport regulation by cloning the first protein that transports this sugar across cell membranes. He also has been a leader in studying the hormones that

As obesity becomes a more common sight in America, scientists are just starting to find biological causes and, possibly, treatments.

fat cells secrete, comments diabetes researcher Jeffrey Flier of Harvard University. . . .

Hormone Deficiency Affects Fat Regulation

For many years, fat cells were seen simply as cells that were . . . well . . . *fat*. That is, nothing more than passive repositories of triglycerides, the chief component of fats and oils. But that assumption took a hit in 1994 when Rockefeller University researcher Jeffrey Friedman discovered a hormone called leptin.

Studying mice that were genetically modified to be obese, Friedman found that leptin acts as a sort of thermostat for fat. When the mice ate too much, fat cells released leptin into the brain, where it would release a series of signals dictating that enough's enough.

Further studies showed that mice who were deficient in leptin couldn't stop eating and would thus become grossly obese. Once they were administered the hormone intravenously, their appetites returned to normal.

As it turns out, a small percentage of people are leptin-deficient and can be treated the same way. Undoubtedly, leptin is a "good" hormone.

But here's the real kicker: Friedman had found that leptin was produced *by* fat cells. So fat cells were no longer seen as inert units for triglyceride storage. They were active players secreting important metabolic hormones.

The following year, the Lodish lab made an equally startling discovery when it found another fat-cell-secreted hormone called adiponectin, which acts in concert with insulin in helping the cells to absorb glucose from the blood. Adiponectin also helps the body to burn off fat and sugar by stimulating the same chemical pathway that is activated when we exercise.

"Clearly," says Lodish, "adiponectin is a good thing to have." The real power of adiponectin became clear in a paper that Lodish and co-workers published in the journal *Proceedings from the National Academy of Sciences*, in 2001. Here, the researchers studied a group of mice that had been made obese through what Lodish refers to as a "cafeteria diet."

A cafeteria diet is exactly what it sounds like. These mice were fed all the butter and sugar they wanted—and their desire knew no limit. Once the mice were suitably obese, Lodish and his team injected them with adiponectin. The mice in turn increased their "burning" of the stored fat and lost weight—results that appeared to be almost miraculous.

Young people participate in a school exercise program aimed at reducing obesity and its health risks in children.

"We tried to publish this in one of the major journals but couldn't because the reviewers simply didn't believe it," Lodish recalls. "The fact that injecting adiponectin caused these mice to increase the burning of fatty acids was just too startling. Once we got it published I had to keep reminding the media over and over again how mice aren't people. Many scientists didn't believe our work until it was confirmed by two other labs the following fall."

Adiponectin is a great hormone to have in abundance, and it's a terrible hormone to lack. Rare genetic conditions that cause adiponectin deficiency may cause diabetes and heart trouble. But here's where things get counterintuitive.

If leptin and adiponectin are manufactured by fat cells, and if having them in abundance is beneficial, then doesn't it stand to reason that the bigger you are, the more of these hormones you produce, and thus the healthier you should be? Isn't there some kind of bigness benefit?

By manipulating its genes, scientists have created an obese mouse (left). Scientists use mice to learn how the body burns fat.

Before you reach for those Super-sized fries, the answer is no. As it turns out, obese people become resistant to leptin. What's more, fat cells in obese tissue start to underproduce adiponectin, so obese people become deficient in this crucial hormone.

Differences in Tissue Composition

Now things get worse. Recent studies comparing fat tissue from normal-weight people and from obese people have provided further evidence that not all fat cells are created equal.

In people with normal weight, fat tissue contains precisely what you'd expect to find: lots of fat cells (known as "adipocytes" in the scientific parlance). But in obese people, fat tissue is loaded with cells called macrophages, cells that normally ingest pathogens and other foreign materials. When they ingest these foreign objects, they release inflammatory hormones that alert the immune system, hormones such as macrophage-produced tumor necrosis factor alpha (TNFa), a hormone that is elevated in arthritis and is also related to cancer and other conditions.

This makes perfect sense, because obesity is essentially an inflammatory disease, comments Gökhan Hotamisligil, professor of genetics and metabolism at the Harvard School of Public Health. "Excess calories affect the fat cells in such a way that they mount an immune response," he says. "You're activating the immune system without a legitimate pathogen," Hotamisligil continues. "You're constantly activating your immune system at a low level in such a way that it releases chemicals that start contributing to inflammation."

Obesity, then, causes stress, which alerts the immune system, which leads to the production of inflammatory mediators that interfere with the function of other metabolic pathways, which in turn causes stress. "It soon turns into a vicious cycle," says Hotamisligil.

Lodish points out that the inflammatory hormone TNFa, which is found abundantly in fat tissue from obese people, blocks the expression of many fat cell genes that are vital for insulin action, including adiponectin (this is why obese people have less adiponectin in their blood).

Hong Ruan, a postdoctoral researcher in Lodish's lab, found that high levels of TNFa alter gene expression in such a way that fewer fatty acids are stored in the fat cells. Instead they are released into the blood, creating insulin resistance in the muscle.

"This process goes on for many years, so eventually you wind up with low levels of adiponectin, high levels of fatty acids in the blood, and high levels of glucose in the blood," says Lodish. But how might all these new insights into the biology of obesity lead toward therapies?

Continuing Obesity Research

Hanging on the wall of Lodish's office, near copies of the best-selling molecular biology textbook he coauthored, is Whitehead's patent on the hormone adiponectin, the molecule responsible for making those obese cafeteria-diet mice lean and mean.

While Lodish may be a hero to the world's millions of rodents, the hormone has yet to work the same kind of magic in people. Serono, the world's largest biotech, ended up acquiring rights to the molecule. And it's apparently hard at work trying to develop an adiponectin product that can be injected into people—perhaps the closest we could ever come to realizing every couch potato's fantasy of losing weight simply by taking your medicine.

"We've recently discovered seven other molecules in the genome that work the same way as adiponectin," adds Lodish. He just signed a licensing agreement with Wyeth Pharmaceuticals to work on these hormones.

The research joins hundreds of other projects shooting for weight-reduction drugs. And even though adiponectin activates the very same metabolic pathways stimulated by exercise, it probably won't be a chocoholic's dream come true. The molecular complexities of fat tissue and the difficulties of production and delivery still pose serious obstacles.

And despite all the research advances, obesity is still in many respects uncharted terrain. "We don't even know yet the location of the genes that very likely make people susceptible to obesity," says Harvard's Flier. "These genes could be active in the brain, or

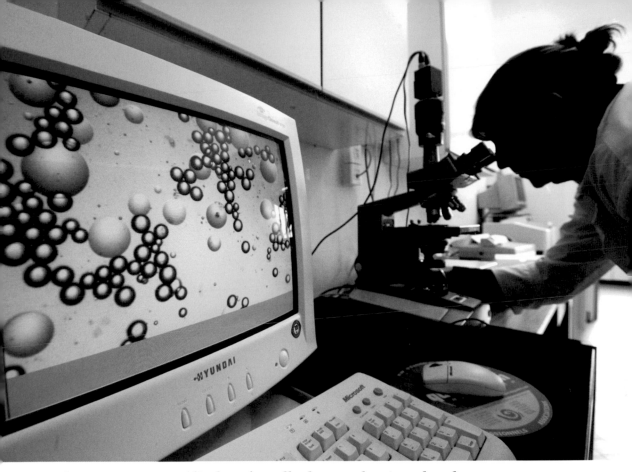

A computer screen displays fat cells that can be viewed under a microscope. Until science discovers the biological causes of obesity, diet and exercise are prescribed.

in the fat cells, or in the muscle cells, or really everywhere." Flier believes that the answer most likely will come from large-scale population studies.

Will there ever be a "cure" for obesity? "It's really too early to say," says Lodish. "I doubt a single molecule will ever do the trick. But one might help reduce the problem, especially in the early stages." In the meantime, here's his prescription: "Diet and exercise."

What You Should Know About Obesity

Obesity is commonly assessed by calculating body mass index (BMI), which is defined as the weight (in kilograms), divided by height (in meters squared). A value higher than twenty-seven indicates mild obesity. A value of thirty or higher indicates more severe obesity.

Determining Your Body Mass Index (BMI)

The table on the following page shows the math and metric conversions. To use the table, find the appropriate height in the left-hand column. Move across the row to the given weight. The number at the top of the column is the BMI for that height and weight. Pounds have been rounded off.

How Prevalent Is Obesity?

- At least 300 million people worldwide suffer from obesity.
- According to the U.S. Bureau of Census, about 58 million adults, or 30 percent of the adult population in the United States, are obese (26 million men and 32 million women).
- Nearly 4 million Americans weigh more than three hundred pounds.
- 17 percent of whites, 27 percent of African Americans, and 21 percent of Latinos are considered obese.
- About two-thirds of all U.S. adults are overweight.
- About 21 percent of teenagers are significantly overweight.
- The number of overweight adolescents in the United States has tripled since 1980.

- About 38 percent of European children are overweight or obese.
- In England adult obesity rates have tripled and the rates in children have doubled since 1982.
- The obesity rates for Canadian children tripled from the 1980s through the 1990s and continue to rise.
- About 10 percent of children in China are overweight, and the number is increasing by 8 percent every year.
- The number of overweight Japanese has more than quadrupled since 1970.

Body Mass Index

BMI	19	20	21	22	23	24	25	26	27	28	29	30	31	32	33	34	35
58	91	96	100	105	110	115	119	124	129	134	138	143	148	153	158	162	167
59	94	99	104	109	114	119	124	128	133	138	143	148	153	158	163	168	173
60	97	102	107	112	118	123	128	133	138	143	148	153	158	163	168	174	179
61	100	106	111	116	122	127	132	137	143	148	153	158	164	169	174	180	185
62	104	109	115	120	126	131	136	142	147	153	158	164	169	175	180	186	191
63	107	113	118	124	130	135	141	146	152	158	163	169	175	180	186	191	197
64	110	116	122	128	134	140	145	151	157	163	169	174	180	186	192	197	204
65	114	120	126	132	138	144	150	156	162	168	174	180	186	192	198	204	210
66	118	124	130	136	142	148	155	161	167	173	179	186	192	198	204	210	216
67	121	127	134	140	146	153	159	166	172	178	185	191	198	204	211	217	223
68	125	131	138	144	151	158	164	171	177	184	190	197	203	210	216	223	230
69	128	135	142	149	155	162	169	176	182	189	196	203	209	216	223	230	236
70	132	139	146	153	160	167	174	181	188	195	202	209	216	222	229	236	243
71	136	143	150	157	165	172	179	186	193	200	208	215	222	229	236	243	250
72	140	147	154	162	169	177	184	191	199	206	213	221	228	235	242	250	258
73	144	151	159	166	174	182	189	197	204	212	219	227	235	242	250	257	265
74	148	155	163	171	179	186	194	202	210	218	225	233	241	249	256	264	272
75	152	160	168	176	184	192	200	208	216	224	232	240	248	256	264	272	279
76	156	164	172	180	189	197	205	213	221	230	238	246	254	263	271	279	287

Height (inches)

Body Weight (pounds)

* Note that BMI has some limitations. It can incorrectly classify healthy, muscular people as overweight because muscle weighs more than fat. In addition, BMI can underestimate the body fat of people who have lost muscle mass.

Source: National Heart, Lung, and Blood Institute, www.nhlbi.nih.gov.

- In South Africa more than 9 percent of men and 29 percent of women are obese.
- Almost 60 percent of the Australian population is overweight or obese.
- Since 1980 obesity rates have more than tripled in some parts of the Middle East.

What Are the Causes of Obesity?

Obesity is caused by people taking in more calories or energy than their bodies burn. These calories are stored as fat. However, there is great debate over why more people are becoming obese. Some of the arguments are listed below.

- People are eating more meals at fast-food restaurants, which typically contain nearly twice the calories of a home-cooked meal.
- The portion sizes served in restaurants and sold in packages have increased sharply since the 1980s.
- The American workplace has changed, with more people performing sedentary desk jobs than in decades past. As a result, they are expending less energy and gaining weight.
- The number of hours people spend on sedentary activities such as watching TV, playing video games, and working on the computer has increased. Forty-three percent of adolescents watch more than two hours of television every day.
- While people are consuming more food, they are also engaging in less physical activity and exercise. Less than one-third of U.S. adults get regular physical activity, defined by the U.S. Department of Agriculture as any activity that requires the energy it takes to walk about two miles in half an hour.
- About 25 percent of young people (aged twelve to twenty-one) do no vigorous physical activity.
- Lower-income earners have a hard time affording fresh, nutritious foods and instead buy cheaper, higher calorie items.
- Some compulsive overeaters eat to soothe emotions such as anxiety, fear, boredom, and sadness.

- Drugs that cause weight gain, including corticosteroids and many antidepressants, are increasingly being prescribed by doctors.
- Scientists have discovered that genes influence how efficiently the body burns calories for energy and how much fat the body stores.
- Thyroid gland problems are an uncommon cause of obesity.

How Does Obesity Affect Health?

People who are overweight or obese are more likely to develop the following health problems:

- cancer
- type 2 diabetes
- fatigue
- carpal tunnel syndrome
- gallstones
- GERD (gastroesophageal reflux disease)
- heart disease
- high cholesterol
- hypertension
- insomnia
- kidney disease
- liver disease
- varicose veins
- degenerative arthritis
- birth defects
- female infertility
- restricted mobility
- sleep apnea and other breathing problems
- strokes
- surgical complications
- back problems
- urinary stress incontinence
- depression

- About three hundred thousand deaths every year in the United States are linked to overweight and obesity.

- The annual health-care costs of American adults with obesity are approximately $100 billion.
- Obese children are developing diseases and disorders previously believed to be limited to adults, including type 2 diabetes and heart disease.
- Overweight adolescents have a 70 percent chance of becoming overweight or obese adults.
- Approximately 90 percent of people with type 2 diabetes are obese or overweight.
- People who have a BMI of thirty or above face a 50 percent increase in the risk of death related to obesity.

What You Should Do About Obesity

Before trying to lose weight, talk with a parent, doctor, or registered dietician. They can help you to come up with a safe weight loss plan that is based on exercise and good nutrition. Starving or crash diets usually do not work and will leave you feeling tired. Instead, aim to lose weight gradually, at a rate of about one-half to two pounds per week. If you reduced your caloric intake by only two hundred calories a day, you would lose about two pounds a month, or twenty pounds a year. Keep in mind that losing a significant amount of weight is only appropriate if you are overweight. Normal-weight individuals should not undertake such a reduction plan.

Keeping a Food Diary

It may help you to keep a food diary in which you keep track of everything you eat and drink for one month, including small snacks. Note the time of day you eat, where you eat, the amount, and how you are feeling. At the end of the month, review your food diary, looking for patterns in your eating habits. For example, do you eat more when you are feeling stressed or bored? Do you skip breakfast? Do you pack lunches or end up buying fast food?

Your food diary will likely reveal a few unhealthy eating habits. Choose one of these habits to change at a time, since making many changes at once can be overwhelming. If you find yourself eating sweet snacks in the afternoon for energy, for instance, you may want to try to eat a healthier, high protein snack instead. Although snacks high in sugar and carbohydrates can provide an instant burst of energy, they cause blood sugar to drop, leaving you feeling hungrier and more tired afterward.

Once you have changed one unhealthy habit, choose another one to change. It is easier to set small goals rather than try to overhaul all of your eating habits at once.

You may also want to attend a support group to help with weight reduction—you can check with your local hospital or the health section of a newspaper to find groups nearby.

Tips for Healthier Eating

In order to lose weight safely without depriving your body of vital nutrients needed for health, use the Food Guide Pyramid developed by the U.S. Department of Agriculture as a starting point. Choose the recommended number of daily servings from each of the five major food groups.

Food Guide Pyramid

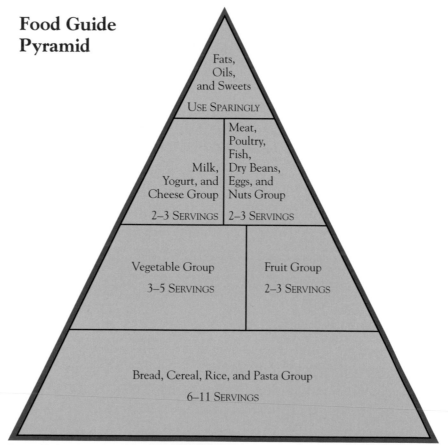

Fats,
Oils,
and Sweets

USE SPARINGLY

Milk,
Yogurt, and
Cheese Group

2–3 SERVINGS

Meat,
Poultry,
Fish,
Dry Beans,
Eggs, and
Nuts Group

2–3 SERVINGS

Vegetable Group

3–5 SERVINGS

Fruit Group

2–3 SERVINGS

Bread, Cereal, Rice, and Pasta Group

6–11 SERVINGS

Source: U.S. Department of Agriculture/U.S. Department of Health and Human Services.

What Counts as a Serving?

Bread, Cereal, Rice, and Pasta Group (Grains Group)— Whole Grain and Refined

- 1 slice of bread
- About 1 cup of ready-to-eat cereal
- ½ cup of cooked cereal, rice, or pasta

Vegetable Group

- 1 cup of raw leafy vegetables
- ½ cup of other vegetables, cooked or raw
- ¾ cup of vegetable juice

Fruit Group

- 1 medium apple, banana, orange, or pear
- ½ cup of chopped, cooked, or canned fruit
- ¾ cup of fruit juice

Milk, Yogurt, and Cheese Group (Milk Group)*

- 1 cup of milk** or yogurt**
- 1½ ounces of natural cheese** (such as cheddar)
- 2 ounces of processed cheese** (such as American)

Meat, Poultry, Fish, Dry Beans, Eggs, and Nuts Group (Meat and Beans Group)

- 2–3 ounces of cooked lean meat, poultry, or fish
- ½ cup of cooked dry beans# or ½ cup of tofu counts as 1 ounce of lean meat
- 2½-ounce soy burger or 1 egg counts as 1 ounce of lean meat
- 2 tablespoons of peanut butter or ⅓ cup of nuts counts as 1 ounce of meat

NOTE: Many of the serving sizes given above are smaller than those on the Nutrition Facts Label. For example, 1 serving of cooked cereal, rice, or pasta is 1 cup for the label but only ½ cup for the Pyramid.

 * This includes lactose-free and lactose-reduced milk products. One cup of soy-based beverage with added calcium is an option for those who prefer a nondairy source of calcium.

** Choose fat-free or reduced-fat dairy products most often.

 # Dry beans, peas, and lentils can be counted as servings in either the meat and beans group or the vegetable group. As a vegetable, ½ cup of cooked, dry beans counts as 1 serving. As a meat substitute, 1 cup of cooked, dry beans counts as 1 serving (2 ounces of meat).

Source: Adapted from U.S. Department of Agriculture, Center for Nutrition Policy and Promotion.

Further Suggestions for Weight Loss

- Eat breakfast every day.
- Cut the amount of fatty and sugary foods in your diet. High-fat foods contain more calories than the same quantity of other foods. However, low-fat foods do not necessarily have low calories. Food manufacturers may add extra sugar to low-fat muffins or dessert, for example, making them as high in calories as the regular versions.
- Avoid processed foods and snacks such as chips and candy. Instead, try a piece of whole-grain toast or a small portion of pretzels.
- Limit the amount of fast food you eat and order small portions.
- Drink fat-free or low-fat milk or water instead of soft drinks and fruit juices, which are loaded with sugar and calories.
- Eat slowly because it takes several minutes for the brain to register that the stomach is full.
- Avoid eating while watching television or reading as you are likely to eat more than you intend to.
- Check product labels to see how much food is considered a serving. Many products marketed as a single portion actually contain two or more servings, such as a twenty-ounce soft drink, a three-ounce bag of chips, or a sixteen-ounce can of soup.
- Do not eat if you are not hungry. Often people eat to soothe emotions such as sadness or anger rather than out of physical hunger.

Engage in Regular Physical Activity

In order to lose weight, your body needs to burn off more calories than it consumes. The best way to burn off extra calories is to do regular physical activities or sports. Exercise raises the metabolism and makes you feel more energetic. According to some obesity research, increasing physical activity and eating healthfully is a much more effective way to lose weight than dieting.

- Do moderate physical activity for at least thirty minutes five times a week.
- Alternate activities so you do not get bored and lose interest. You do not have to join a gym to get exercise. Running, skating, dancing, biking, and brisk walking are excellent forms of exercise.

- Even small changes in your daily habits can help to prevent obesity:
  - Take the stairs instead of the elevator.
  - Park your car at the far end of the parking lot and walk the extra distance.
  - Limit the time spent watching television and playing video games.
  - Walk or bike places instead of driving.
  - Get off the bus a few stops early and walk the extra distance.

Weight Loss Surgery

In the case of severe obesity, some people choose to undergo gastric bypass or bariatric surgery, in which the surgeon creates a small pouch in the stomach to receive food, making it difficult to consume large amounts of food. Immediately after the surgery, patients are only able to eat a few tablespoons of food before feeling full. After the first year, they can consume about five ounces of food at a time. The cost of bariatric surgery ranges from twenty thousand dollars to fifty thousand dollars. Medical insurance coverage varies by state and by insurance provider.

Gastric bypass surgery is a drastic measure that you should consider only if you have repeatedly tried to lose weight without success. The clinical guidelines for the surgery state that a patient should have a body mass index of forty or greater or weigh more than one hundred pounds over ideal body weight. In addition, if obesity is aggravating serious health conditions such as diabetes or heart disease, weight loss surgery may be considered.

If you are thinking about undergoing gastric bypass surgery, you should consider the following risks and benefits:

Risks

Approximately 30 percent of gastric bypass patients develop nutritional deficiencies, including anemia, osteoporosis, and metabolic bone disease.

- Some patients develop gallstones, which are clumps of cholesterol and other matter that form in the gallbladder that often need to be surgically removed.
- About 10 to 20 percent of patients require follow-up procedures to correct complications.
- Studies show that one in three hundred patients die from gastric bypass surgery.
- Some patients develop food intolerances, especially to red meat, sugar, and milk, and experience nausea and vomiting.
- Some patients experience hair loss because of protein malnutrition.

Other complications include lung collapse, blood clots in the legs, wound infection, fluid collection in the abdomen, abdominal hernias, and the formation of scar tissue.

Benefits

After surgery most patients lose weight quickly and continue to lose weight for about two years after the procedure.

- Many patients lose 100 to 200 pounds or more. In contrast, people who take weight loss drugs or go on diets lose an average of about only 10 percent of their body weight, which is only 40 pounds for someone who weighs 400 pounds.
- Research shows that ten years after gastric bypass surgery, patients have maintained an average loss of 60 percent of their excess weight.
- Bypass surgery can help to alleviate high blood pressure, sleep apnea, and diabetes associated with obesity.

Other Recommendations

People considering gastric bypass surgery should talk with other people who have undergone the surgery to get a firsthand account of what they may expect. It is also extremely important to interview surgeons and find out how many weight-loss surgery procedures they have performed and what the outcomes of these procedures have been.

American Council for Fitness and Nutrition (ACFN)
PO Box 33396, Washington, DC 20033-3396
(800) 953-1700
Web site: www.acfn.org

The ACFN describes itself as "a non-profit organization that brings together food and beverage companies, associations, and health and nutrition advocates to work toward viable long-term solutions to the nation's obesity epidemic." The organization provides information to health specialists, educators, and policy makers with the goal of improving the health and well-being of the public. The ACFN publishes the newsletter *Food for Thought*.

American Obesity Association (AOA)
1250 Twenty-fourth St. NW, Suite 300, Washington, DC 20037
(202) 776-7711
fax: (202) 776-7712
Web site: www.obesity.org

AOA works to advance new treatments for obesity, lobbies for improved health care and insurance coverage, fights discrimination against the obese, and supports the obese community. The AOA publishes a newsletter that is primarily distributed as an e-newsletter to AOA members and posted on its Web site.

American Psychiatric Association (APA)
1000 Wilson Blvd., Suite 1825, Arlington, VA 22209-3901
(703) 907-7300
e-mail: apa@psych.org
Web site: www.psych.org

APA is an organization of psychiatrists dedicated to studying the nature, treatment, and prevention of mental disorders. It helps create mental-health policies, distributes information about psychiatry, and promotes psychiatric research and education. APA publishes the monthly *American Journal of Psychiatry*. American

Psychiatric Publishing Inc. is a subsidiary of the APA that distributes books on a number of health issues. The APA also provides links to numerous fact sheets and brochures on topics such as eating disorders and depression on its HealthyMinds.org Web site.

American Psychological Association (APA)
750 First St. NE, Washington, DC 20002-4242
(202) 336-5500
fax: (202) 336-5708
e-mail: public.affairs@apa.org
Web site: www.apa.org

The stated aim of the APA is to "advance psychology as a science, as a profession, and as a means of promoting human welfare." The organization produces numerous publications, including the monthly journal *American Psychologist*, the monthly newspaper *APA Monitor*, and the quarterly *Journal of Abnormal Psychology*. The APA publishes a number of books and journals that can be browsed by topic at www.apa.org/publications. Two books published by the APA that may be of particular interest to those researching obesity are *Body Image, Eating Disorders, and Obesity* and *Exacting Beauty*.

Centers for Disease Control and Prevention (CDC)
1600 Clifton Rd., Atlanta, GA 30333
(404) 639-3311
Web site: www.cdc.gov

The stated mission of the CDC is to "prevent and control infectious and chronic diseases, injuries, workplace hazards, disabilities, and environmental health threats." The CDC is a popular source for information and statistics on the obesity problem in the United States. It also funds a number of programs about health, fitness, and nutrition, such as Coordinated School Health Programs and STEPS to a Healthier US. The CDC prepares the *Morbidity and Mortality Weekly Report* based on information gathered from state health departments. The CDC also publishes an electronic journal called *Preventing Chronic Disease*. A full list of CDC publications is available on its Web site.

Food and Drug Administration (FDA)
5600 Fishers Ln., Rockville, MD 20857
(888) INFO-FDA
(888) 463-6332
Web site: www.fda.gov

The Food and Drug Administration is responsible for ensuring the public's health through the regulation of drugs, medical devices, cosmetics, and other products in the United States. The FDA also regulates food labeling and evaluates the safety of food products. The *FDA Consumer*, the official magazine of the FDA, is published six times a year.

The Food Trust
1201 Chestnut St., 4th Fl., Philadelphia, PA 19107
(215) 568-0830
fax: (215) 568-0882
Web site: www.thefoodtrust.org

The Food Trust works to promote better access to healthy foods, improve the health of the public, and advance public policy. It sponsors a number of school and community-based programs that seek to increase the availability of nutritious food. Two such programs are School Food and Beverage Reform and the Corner Store Campaign, both of which seek to reduce rates of obesity by providing healthier food choices for children and adolescents. The Food Trust publishes a newsletter called *Food Matters*.

National Association to Advance Fat Acceptance (NAAFA)
PO Box 22510, Oakland, CA 94609
(916) 558-6880
Web site: www.naafa.org

NAAFA is an organization committed to providing obese people with equal opportunities, fighting discrimination, and advocating the acceptance of obese people in society. It urges people to accept their weight and live their lives to the fullest. NAAFA has over fifty local chapters across the United States, holds an annual convention, and publishes *NAAFA Newsletter* as well as numerous informative brochures on its Web site.

National Eating Disorder Information Centre (NEDIC)

ES 7-421, 200 Elizabeth St., Toronto, ON M5G 2C4 Canada
(416) 340-4156
fax: (416) 340-4736
e-mail: mbeck@torhosp.toronto.on.ca
Web site: www.nedic.ca

NEDIC provides information and resources on eating disorders and weight preoccupation, focusing on the sociocultural factors that influence female health-related behaviors. NEDIC promotes healthy lifestyles and encourages people to make informed choices based on accurate information. It publishes a variety of materials, which can be found through its Web site, for people who suffer from eating disorders and their families and friends. The organization also sponsors Eating Disorders Awareness Week in Canada.

National Eating Disorders Association (NEDA)
(formerly the National Eating Disorders Organization)

603 Stewart St., Suite 803, Seattle, WA 98101
(206) 382-3587
Web site: www.nationaleatingdisorders.org

NEDA provides information, prevention, and treatment resources for all forms of eating disorders. The organization believes that eating disorders are multidimensional, developed and sustained by biological, social, psychological, and familial factors. It publishes information packets, a video, and a newsletter and holds a semiannual national conference.

Society for Adolescent Medicine (SAM)

1916 NW Copper Oaks Circle, Blue Springs, MO 64015
(816) 224-8010
fax: (816) 224-8009
e-mail: sam@adolescenthealth.org
Web site: www.adolescenthealth.org

SAM is a multidisciplinary organization of professionals committed to improving the physical and psychological health and well-being of all adolescents. It helps plan and coordinate national and international professional education programs on adolescent health. Its publications include the monthly *Journal of Adolescent Health* and the quarterly *SAM Newsletter*.

United States Department of Agriculture (USDA)
1400 Independence Ave. SW, Washington, DC 20250
Web site: www.usda.gov

The United States Department of Agriculture sponsors research on nutrition and manages the food stamp, school lunch, school breakfast, and WIC programs. The goals of its Food and Nutrition Service are to provide low-income families with access to healthy foods and education on nutrition. The USDA's Center for Nutrition Policy and Promotion develops dietary guidelines. Its publications include *Food and Nutrition Research Briefs* and *Food Review*.

Weight-Control Information Network (WIN)
1 WIN Way, Bethesda, MD 20892-3665
(877) 946-4627
fax: (202) 828-1028
e-mail: win@info.niddk.nih.gov
Web site: www.win.niddk.nih.gov

WIN is an information service of the National Institute of Diabetes and Digestive and Kidney Diseases at the National Institutes of Health. It offers the public information regarding obesity, nutrition, physical activity, and issues surrounding weight control. The organization also provides publications, fact sheets, videos, and abstracts of books and periodicals that cover health and nutrition issues. Publications of interest include *Helping Your Overweight Child*, *Physical Activity and Weight Control*, and *Choosing a Safe and Successful Weight-Loss Program*, all of which are available through the WIN Web site.

BIBLIOGRAPHY

Books

Bouchard, Claude, ed., *Physical Activity and Obesity*. Champaign, IL: Human Kinetics, 2000.

Brownell, Kelly, and Katherine Battle Horgen, *Food Fight: The Inside Story of the Food Industry, America's Obesity Crisis, and What We Can Do About It*. Chicago: Contemporary Books, 2004.

Campbell, Ian W., and David W. Haslam, *Obesity: Your Questions Answered*. Edinburgh: Churchill Livingstone, 2005.

Crister, Greg, *Fat Land*. New York: Houghton Mifflin, 2003.

Dalton, Sharron, *Our Overweight Children: What Parents, Schools, and Communities Can Do to Control the Fatness Epidemic*. Berkeley and Los Angeles: University of California Press, 2004.

Knight, Joseph A., *A Crisis Call for New Preventive Medicine: Emerging Effects of Lifestyle on Morbidity and Mortality*. River Edge, NJ: World Scientific, 2004.

Kulick, Don, and Anne Meneley, *Fat: The Anthropology of an Obsession*. New York: Jeremy P. Tarcher/Penguin, 2005.

Ogden, Jane, *The Psychology of Eating: From Healthy to Disordered Behavior*. Malden, MA: Blackwell, 2003.

Okie, Susan, *Fed Up! Winning the War Against Childhood Obesity*. Washington, DC: Joseph Henry, 2005.

Oliver, J. Eric, *Fat Politics: The Real Story Behind America's Obesity Epidemic*. New York: Oxford University Press, 2006.

Pool, Robert, *Fat: Fighting the Obesity Epidemic*. New York: Oxford University Press, 2001.

Schlosser, Eric, *Fast Food Nation*. New York: Houghton Mifflin, 2002.

Sobal, Jeffery, and Donna Maurer, eds., *Weighty Issues: Fatness and Thinness as Social Problem*. New York: Aldine de Gruyter, 1999.

Wadden, Thomas A., *Handbook of Obesity Treatment*. New York: Guilford, 2002.

Wann, Marilyn, *FAT!SO? Because You Don't Have to Apologize for Your Size*. Berkeley, CA: Ten Speed Press, 1998.

Periodicals

Anderson, Harvey, "Come Eat with Me," *New Scientist*, vol. 187, August 6, 2005.

Boyle, Matthew, "Can You Really Make Fast Food Healthy?" *Fortune*, vol. 150, August 9, 2004.

Brink, Susan, and Elizabeth Querna, "Eat This Now!" *U.S. News & World Report*, vol. 38, March 28, 2005.

Butryn, Meghan, and Thomas Wadden, "Treatment of Overweight in Children and Adolescents: Does Dieting Increase the Risk of Eating Disorders?" *International Journal of Eating Disorders*, vol. 37, May 2005.

Cordes, Helen, "Fat Cities," *Sierra*, vol. 90, January/February 2005.

Couzin, Jennifer, "Fat Under Attack," *Science Now*, June 20, 2005.

Gibbs, W. Wayt, "Obesity: An Overblown Epidemic?" *Scientific American*, vol. 293, June 2005.

Gorman, Christine, and Coco Masters, "Is It O.K. to Be Pudgy?" *Time*, vol. 165, May 9, 2005.

Johnson, Patrick, "Obesity: Epidemic or Myth?" *Skeptical Inquirer*, September/October 2003.

Jones, Rachel, "When Dieting Doesn't Work," *Essence*, vol. 35, August 2004.

MacDonald, Pat, "The Obesity Crisis . . . It's Not Just About Diets," *Practice Nurse*, vol. 29, April 29, 2005.

Miller, Wayne C., "Exercise and Weight: Fit or Fat or Fit and Fat?" *Health at Every Size*, vol. 19, Summer 2005.

Motluk, Alison, "Supersize Me," *New Scientist*, vol. 184, October 20, 2004.

Munro, Neil, "Growing Fat on Obesity," *National Journal,* vol. 37, February 29, 2005.

Packard, R. Andrew, "A Girth of Problems," *American Fitness,* vol. 23, March/April 2005.

Pennisi, Elizabeth, "Getting Fat? Blame Your Gut Bugs," *Science Now,* November 4, 2004.

Rashad, Inas, and Michael Grossman, "The Economics of Obesity," *Public Interest,* Summer 2004.

Sklaroff, Sara, "How America Eats," *U.S. News & World Report,* vol. 139, August 15, 2005.

Skloot, Rebecca, "Flabby Coverage," *Popular Science,* vol. 267, July 2005.

Sullum, Jacob, "The War on Fat," *Reason,* vol. 36, August/September 2004.

Tillotson, James E., "The Heavy Burden of Eating Out Today," *Nutrition Today,* vol. 40, July/August 2005.

Underwood, Anne, and Jerry Adler, "What You Don't Know About Fat," *Newsweek,* vol. 144, August 23, 2004.

Witt, Louise, "Why We're Losing the War Against Obesity," *American Demographics,* vol. 25, December 2003/January 2004.

ABOUT THE EDITOR

Erin Dillon is a freelance writer living in Athens, Ohio. She received her bachelor's degree from the E.W. Scripps School of Journalism at Ohio University.